Jones

T3-BWQ-385

$5.50

CRIMINAL LAW
FOR
THE POLICE

Inbau Law Enforcement Series

CRIMINAL LAW
FOR
THE POLICE

FRED E. INBAU *and* MARVIN E. ASPEN

CHILTON BOOK COMPANY

PHILADELPHIA   NEW YORK   LONDON

Published in Philadelphia by Chilton Book Company
and simultaneously in Ontario, Canada,
by Thomas Nelson & Sons, Ltd.

Library of Congress Catalog Card Number 70-97963

ISBN 0-8019-5413-4

Designed by William E. Lickfield

Manufactured in the United States of America

Preface

This book has been prepared to meet a very essential need in the field of law enforcement. Today, more than ever before, a knowledge of the fundamentals of criminal law and criminal procedure is indispensable to the effective performance of the duties of a law enforcement officer.

Part I of this book presents an *Outline of Criminal Procedure.* Part II deals with *Crimes,* in which an effort has been made to define and explain the various legal prohibitions with respect to offensive behavior toward other human beings and their property. Part III is devoted to *The Legal Rules Governing Police Practices and Procedures.* Part IV discusses *The Criminal and Civil Liability of Law Enforcement Officers.*

In an Appendix we have reproduced certain provisions of the Constitution of the United States and its Amendments that are of particular importance to law enforcement officers. This we have done because an officer, although he frequently hears of such constitutional rights of free speech, due process, and the self-incrimination privilege, may never have had the opportunity to examine the various constitutional provisions themselves.

FRED E. INBAU
MARVIN E. ASPEN

To JANE ———
  from F.E.I.
To SUE ———
  from M.E.A.

Contents

PART II. CRIMES

PART III. THE LEGAL RULES GOVERNING POLICE
          PRACTICES AND PROCEDURES

PART IV. CRIMINAL AND CIVIL LIABILITY OF LAW ENFORCEMENT OFFICERS

APPENDICES

Part I

OUTLINE OF
CRIMINAL PROCEDURE

Outline of Criminal Procedure

Early in his career a police officer will be placed in the position of a participant in the judicial process as it relates to criminal offenses. One of his first arrests may result in his appearance in court as a witness. Without some acquaintance with criminal procedure, his early courtroom experiences will most certainly be bewildering; in fact, those limited experiences may prevent an adequate understanding of what he sees or hears in the courtroom. We begin this book, therefore, with an outline and general explanation of the legal procedures involved in a criminal case, stated in as non-legalistic a way as circumstances permit.

Another of the officer's early encounters will be with the legal controls imposed upon his police functions by provisions in both federal and state constitutions. He will hear of freedom of speech, the self-incrimination privilege, due process, and other constitutional guarantees, but he may never have seen the various provisions themselves. We have considered it appropriate, therefore, to reproduce those portions of the Constitution of the United States and its Amendments which are of special importance to the police officer. (See Appendix.) For obvious reasons, it is impractical to attempt this on the state level. Moreover, there is no necessity to do so, because 1) the relevant state constitutional provisions closely parallel those of the Federal Constitution, and 2) many federal constitutional provisions that were formerly considered applicable only to federal proceedings are now interpreted as binding on the states as well.

Although the court procedure followed in criminal cases is not uniform among the fifty states, the differences with respect to basic concepts and principles are rather slight. Then, too, there is very little basic difference between the procedure used in the state courts and that within the federal system. The following outline fairly typifies the procedure that prevails in the various states and on the federal level*:

1. PROCEDURE BETWEEN ARREST AND TRIAL

In most states there is a statutory provision to the effect that an arrested person must be taken without unnecessary delay before the nearest judge or magistrate. What happens after presentation to the judge or magistrate will depend upon whether the arrested person is accused of a felony or a misdemeanor. (A felony is generally defined as an offense for which the penalty is incarceration for one year or more, usually in a penitentiary; a misdemeanor is an offense punishable up to one year, and usually served in a county jail.)

If the charge against the arrestee is for a misdemeanor, the judge or magistrate will sometimes have the power and authority to hear the case himself, and he will usually proceed with the trial unless the accused demands trial by jury or a continuance is requested or ordered for some reason. If the offense charged is more serious, a felony, the judge or magistrate before whom the accused is first brought will ordinarily lack the constitutional or legislative authority to conduct trial. In such an instance, he conducts a "preliminary hearing".

(a) Preliminary Hearing

This is a relatively informal proceeding by means of which a determination is made as to whether there are reasonable grounds for believing that the accused committed the offense—as to whether it is fair, under the circumstances, to require the accused to stand a regular trial. If after such a hearing the judge or magistrate decides that the accusation is without probable cause, the accused will be discharged. This discharge, however, will not bar a grand jury indictment if subsequently developed evidence (or the same evidence pre-

* This outline is reproduced, with some modification, from the law school casebook, *Cases and Comments on Criminal Justice*, by Fred E. Inbau, James R. Thompson, and Claude R. Sowle (3d ed. 1968), published by Foundation Press, Mineola, New York 11501. That casebook is recommended to police school instructors as a companion text, since it develops, in detail, the principles presented in this book.

sented on the preliminary hearing) satisfies the grand jury that the accusation is well founded.

If the preliminary hearing judge or magistrate decides that the accusation is a reasonable one, the accused will be "bound over" to the grand jury—that is, held in jail until the charge against him is presented for grand jury consideration, or, if the offense is a bailable one, the accused may be released after a bond of a certain amount is given to insure his presence until the grand jury has acted in the matter. (The nature and composition of a "grand jury" and the difference between it and a "petit" or "trial jury" are described later in this outline.)

(b) The Habeas Corpus Writ

In the event an arrested person is not formally charged with an offense and is not taken before a judge or other magistrate "without unnecessary delay" he, or rather someone on his behalf, may petition a judge for a "writ of habeas corpus" and thereby attempt to release him or at least compel the police to file a specific charge against him, in which latter event he may seek his release on bond. If the court issues the writ, the police or other custodians of the arrested person are required, either immediately or at an early designated time, to bring him into court (that is, "you have the body," which is the literal meaning of the term "habeas corpus"), and to explain to the court the reason or justification for holding the accused person in custody.

Upon the police showing adequate cause, a court may continue the hearing in order to give the police a little more time to conduct a further investigation before making the formal charge against the arrestee. Many times, however, the police are required to file their charges immediately or release the prisoner.

(c) Coroner's Inquest

At this point in a discussion of criminal procedure, mention should be made of a proceeding peculiar to homicide cases, which comes into operation soon after a killing or discovered death. This is the "coroner's inquest".

The coroner's inquest is a very old proceeding and its function was and still is to determine "the cause of death". The verdict of the coroner's jury, which is made up, in some states, of six laymen selected by the coroner or one of his deputies, is not binding on the prosecuting attorney, grand jury or court. In effect, it is merely an advisory finding which can be either accepted or completely ignored. For instance, even though a coroner's jury returns a verdict of "accidental death", a grand jury, either upon its own initiative or upon evidence presented by the prosecutor, may find that death resulted because of someone's criminal act and charge that person with the offense.

(d) The Grand Jury

Misdemeanors are usually prosecuted upon an "information" filed by the prosecuting attorney after he has received and considered the sworn complaint of the victim or of some other person with knowledge of the facts. With regard to felonies, however, many states require that the matter must first be submitted to a "grand jury". Then, after hearing the alleged facts related by the victim or other persons, the grand jury determines whether there are reasonable grounds for proceeding to an actual trial of the person charged.

A grand jury is usually composed of 23 citizen-voters, 16 of whom constitute a quorum. The votes of 12 members are necessary to the return of an "indictment". This indictment is also known as a "true bill".

The consideration of a felony charge by a grand jury is in no sense of the word a trial. Only the state's evidence is presented and considered; the suspected offender is usually not even heard nor is his lawyer present to offer evidence in his behalf.

The primary reason for requiring consideration of felony cases by a grand jury is to offer another safeguard to accused persons against arbitrary action by a prosecuting attorney, for without its indictment there can be no trial in felony cases. The indictment is required even in cases where the person charged has already had a preliminary hearing into the reasonableness of the charges against him.

(e) The Arraignment and Plea

Following an indictment, the next step in felony cases is the appearance of the accused person before a judge who is empowered to try felony cases. The indictment is read to the defendant or the essence of its contents is made known to him; in other words, he is advised of the criminal charges made against him. If he pleads guilty, the judge can sentence him immediately or take the matter under advisement for a decision at an early date. If the accused pleads "not guilty", a date is then set for his actual trial.

In some states, and in the federal system, the defendant may enter a plea of "nolo contendere", a plea which has the same effect as a plea of guilty, except that the admission thereby cannot be used as evidence in any other action.

(f) Pre-trial Motions

After the formal charge has been made against the accused, he may, in advance of trial, seek to terminate the prosecution's case, or at least seek to better prepare his defense, by utilizing a procedure known as making or filing a "motion". A motion is merely a request for a court ruling or order that will afford the defendant the assistance or remedy he is thereby seeking. Some of the more frequently used motions are the following:

Motion to Quash the Indictment: With this motion the defendant may question the legal sufficiency of the indictment. If the court decides that the indictment adequately charges a criminal offense, and that it was obtained in accordance with the prescribed legal procedures, the motion will be overruled; otherwise the indictment will be considered invalid and "quashed".

Even after an indictment has been thus rejected and set aside, the prosecutor may nevertheless proceed to obtain another and proper indictment. Moreover, the prosecution is entitled to appeal from a court order quashing an indictment, since at this stage of the proceedings the defendant has not been placed "in jeopardy"—i.e., his actual guilt or innocence has not been under consideration as yet; consequently a subsequent indictment and trial would not constitute a violation of his constitutional privilege against "double jeopardy".

Motion for a Bill of Particulars: Although the indictment, if valid, will ordinarily contain all the allegations of fact necessary for the defendant to prepare his defense, he may, by a motion for a "bill of particulars", obtain further details respecting the accusation.

Motion for a Change of Venue: A defendant may attempt to avoid trial before a particular judge or in the city, county, or district where the crime occurred by seeking a "change of venue". In instances where this appears to be necessary in order that the defendant may receive a fair trial, the motion for a change of venue will be granted.

Motion to Suppress Evidence: A defendant has the privilege of filing with the court, normally in advance of trial, a "motion to suppress" evidence which he contends has been obtained from him in an unconstitutional manner. The evidence in question may be, on the one hand, a tangible item such as a gun, narcotics, or stolen property or, on the other hand, an intangible item such as a confession. If the court is satisfied that the evidence has been illegally obtained, it will order the evidence suppressed, which means that it cannot be used at the trial. If the court decides that the evidence was lawfully obtained, it is usable against the defendant at the trial.

The Trial

In all states, and in the federal system, the accused is entitled to "a speedy trial." This right to an early trial is guaranteed by the various constitutions, and the constitutional provisions are generally supplemented by legislative enactments particularizing and specifically limiting the pre-trial detention period. In Illinois, for instance, once a person is jailed upon a criminal charge, he must be tried within 120 days, unless the delay has been requested by him or an additional length of time up to 60 days has been allowed by the court to the prosecution for the purpose of obtaining further evidence. If the accused is out on bail, he can demand a trial within 120 days, although in this instance too the court can allow the prosecution an additional 60 days. Unless an accused person is prosecuted within the specified period of time, he must be released and is thereafter immune from prosecution for that offense.

An accused person is also entitled to trial by jury, as a matter of constitutional right. However, he may waive his right to a jury trial and be tried by a judge alone. If the case is tried without a jury, the judge hears the evidence and decides for himself whether the defendant is guilty or not guilty. Where the trial is by a jury, the jury determines the facts and the judge serves more or less as an umpire or referee; it is his function to determine what testimony or evidence is legally "admissible", that is, to decide what should be heard or considered by the jury. But the ultimate decision as to whether the defendant is guilty is one to be made by the jury alone.

(a) Jury Selection

In the selection of the jurors, usually twelve in number, who hear the defendant's case, his attorney as well as the prosecuting attorney are permitted to question a large number who have been chosen for jury service from the list of registered voters. Each lawyer has a certain number of "peremptory challenges" which means that he can arbitrarily refuse to accept as jurors a certain number of those who appear as prospective jurors. In some states, by statutory provision, the defendant in larceny cases has ten such challenges and the state has an equal number; in a murder case the defendant and the state each have twenty peremptory challenges; and in minor criminal cases, such as petit larceny, the challenges are five in number for each side. And in all cases, if any prospective juror's answers to the questions of either attorney reveal a prejudice or bias which prevents him from being a fair and impartial juror, the judge, either on his own initiative or at the suggestion of either counsel, will dismiss that person from jury service. Although the desired result is not always achieved, the purpose of this practice of permitting lawyers to question prospective jurors is to obtain twelve jurors who will be fair to both sides of the case.

(b) Opening Statements

After the jury is selected, both the prosecuting attorney and the defense lawyer are entitled to make "opening statements" in which each outlines what he intends to prove. The purpose of this is to acquaint the jurors with each side of the case, so that it will be easier for them to follow the evidence as it is presented.

(c) The Prosecution's Evidence

After the opening statements the prosecuting attorney produces the prosecution's testimony and evidence. He has the burden of proving the state's case "beyond a reasonable doubt". If at the close of the prosecution's case the judge is of the opinion that reasonable jurors could not conclude that the charge against the defendant has been proved, he will "direct a verdict" of acquittal. That ends the matter and the defendant goes free—forever immune from further prosecution for the crime, just the same as if a jury had heard all the evidence and found him "not guilty".

(d) The Defendant's Evidence

If the court does not direct the jury, at the close of the prosecution's case, to find the defendant not guilty, the defendant may, if he wishes, present evidence in refutation. He himself may or may not testify, and if he chooses not to appear as a witness, the prosecuting attorney is not permitted to comment upon that fact to the jury. The basis for this principle, whereby the defendant is not obligated to speak in his own behalf, is the constitutional privilege which protects a person from self-incrimination.

The prosecution is given an opportunity to rebut the defendant's evidence, if any, and the presentation of testimony usually ends at that point. Then, once more, defense counsel will try to persuade the court to "direct a verdict" in favor of the defendant. If the court decides to let the case go to the jury, the prosecuting attorney and defense counsel make their "closing arguments".

(e) Closing Arguments

In their closing arguments the prosecutor and defense counsel review and analyze the evidence and attempt to persuade the jury to render a verdict favorable to that particular side.

(f) Instructions of the Court to the Jury

After the closing arguments are completed, the judge in most jurisdictions will read and give to the jury certain written instructions as to the legal principles which should be applied to the facts of the case as determined by the jury. The judge also gives the jury certain written forms of possible verdicts. The jury then retires to the jury room where they are given an adequate opportunity to deliberate upon the matter, away from everyone, including the judge himself.

(g) The Verdict of the Jury

When the jurors have arrived at a decision, they advise the bailiff that they have reached a verdict and then return to the court room. The foreman, usually selected by the jurors themselves to serve as their leader and spokesman, announces the verdict of the jury. Insofar as jury participation is concerned, the case is then at an end.

If the verdict is "not guilty" the defendant is free forever from any further prosecution for the crime for which he was tried. If found "guilty", in most types of cases and in most jurisdictions, it becomes the function of the trial judge to fix the sentence within the legislatively prescribed limitations.

In the event the jurors are unable to agree upon a verdict—and it must be unanimous in most states—the jury, commonly referred to as a "hung jury", is discharged and a new trial date may be set for a retrial of the case before another jury.

(h) The Motion for a New Trial

After a verdict of "guilty" there are still certain opportunities provided the defendant to obtain his freedom. He may file a "motion for a new trial", in which he alleges certain "errors" committed in the course of his trial; and if the trial judge agrees, the conviction is set aside and the defendant may be tried again by a new jury and usually before a different judge. Where this motion for a new trial is "overruled" or "denied", the judge will then proceed to sentence the defendant.

(i) The Sentence

In cases tried without a jury, the judge, of course, will determine the sentence to be imposed. In jury cases the practice varies among the states, with most of them following the practice of confining the jury function to a determination of guilt or innocence and permitting the judge to fix the penalty. For the crimes of murder and rape, however, most of the states place both responsibilities upon the jury. The jury will decide whether the penalty is to be death or imprisonment, and if the penalty is imprisonment, the jury will also determine the number of years to be served.

In some states there are statutory provisions which prescribe that upon conviction of a felony the defendant must be sentenced for a specified minimum-maximum term in the penitentiary—for example, 1 year to 10 years for burglary—and the determination of the appropriate time of his release within that period is to be made by a "parole board", whose judgment in that respect is based upon the extent of the convict's rehabilitation, the security risk involved, and similar factors. In many states a judge is permitted to set a minimum-maximum period anywhere within the minimum-maximum term prescribed by the legislature. In other words, the sentence given for grand larceny may be one to ten years, the statutory range, or 1 to 2, 9 to 10, or any other combination between 1 to 10. This minimum-maximum term means that he cannot be released before serving the minimum period, less "time off for good behavior", nor can he be kept in the penitentiary longer than the maximum period, less "time off for good behavior". In between this minimum-maximum period the convict is eligible for "parole", a procedure to be subsequently described.

In instances where imprisonment is fixed at a specified number of years, rather than for an indeterminate period, the law usually pro-

12

Outline of Criminal Procedure

vides that the convicted person must serve one-third of the sentence before becoming eligible for parole.

PROBATION

In certain types of cases, a judge is empowered, by statute, to grant "probation" to a convicted person. This means that instead of sending the defendant to the penitentiary the court permits him to remain at liberty but upon certain conditions prescribed by law and by the judge. His background must first be investigated by a probation officer for the purpose of determining whether he is the kind of person who may have "learned his lesson" by the mere fact of being caught and convicted, or whether he could be rehabilitated outside of prison better than behind prison walls. In other words, would any useful purpose be served for him or society by sending him to prison?

Among the conditions of a defendant's probation, the court may require him to make restitution of money stolen, or reparations to a person he physically injured. Some state statutes provide that for a period of up to six months in misdemeanor cases, and up to five years in felony cases, a defendant on probation will be subjected to the supervision of a probation officer and, in general, must remain on "good behavior" during the period fixed by the court. A failure to abide by the conditions prescribed by the court will subject the defendant to a sentence in the same manner and form as though he had been denied probation and sentenced immediately after his conviction for the offense.

PAROLE

A penitentiary sentence of a specified term or number of years does not necessarily mean that a convicted person will remain in the penitentiary for that particular period of time. Under certain conditions and circumstances he may be released earlier "on parole", which means a release under supervision until the expiration of his sentence or until the expiration of a period otherwise specified by law. For instance, a person sentenced "for life" is, in some states, eligible for release "on parole" at the end of 20 years, with a subsequent 5 year period of parole supervision. One sentenced for a fixed number of years, for example 14 years for murder, may be eligible for parole in some states after he has served one-third that period of time. And a person who has been given an indeterminate minimum-maximum sentence, such as 5 to 10 years for grand larceny, may be eligible for a parole after he has served the 5 year minimum, less time off for good behavior.

The manner of computing time off for good behavior, or "good time", varies among the states. Illinois has a system based on yearly credits; under this arrangement, the amount of the credit granted increases as the amount of time served by the obedient prisoner increases. Accordingly, one month off is granted for good behavior in the first year, two months for the second year, and so on up to a maximum of six months off for good behavior in the sixth year and for good behavior in each succeeding year. The inmate is allowed to accumulate these credits. Thus, under the Illinois system, a prisoner who received a minimum-maximum sentence of 3 to 5 years and who served "good time", would be eligible for parole after serving 2 years and 6 months of his sentence.

A violation of the conditions of the parole will subject the parolee to possible return to prison for the remainder of his unexpired sentence.

Post-Conviction Remedies

(a) The Appeal

After sentence has been pronounced, the defendant may appeal his conviction to a reviewing court. The reviewing court will examine all or part of the written record of what happened at the trial, and consider the written and oral arguments of both the defense attorney and the prosecutor. It will then render a written decision and opinion which will either reverse or affirm the trial court conviction and state the reasons for the decision. If the trial court's decision is "reversed and remanded", it means that the defendant's conviction is nullified, although he may be tried over again by another jury. A decision of "reversed" ordinarily means that in addition to an improper trial there appears to be insufficient competent evidence upon which to try the defendant again, and consequently the prosecuting attorney may not make a second attempt to win a conviction.

A decision of the state's highest court affirming a conviction is, in nearly all instances, a final disposition of the case, and there is nothing else the convicted person can do but submit to the judgment of the trial court. But if the appeal involved a *federal* constitutional question or issue the defendant is entitled to seek a review of the state appellate court decision by the Supreme Court of the United

States. Such requests, known as petitions for a *writ of certiorari*, are rarely granted, however.

(b) Collateral Attacks

In addition to the appeal itself, nearly all states in recent years have provided additional post-conviction remedies by which a defendant may attack his conviction. Such "collateral" remedies are known, variously, as proceedings in habeas corpus, post-conviction petitions, or by other titles. A defendant may thereby seek a relitigation, in a trial court, of an issue that had been considered and decided on the direct appeal; or he may attempt to raise an entirely new issue. Moreover, the decision with respect to a collateral attack may be the subject of an appeal to a reviewing court.

Even after a conviction is upheld against collateral attack in the state courts, if a federal constitutional question had been presented, the convicted person has yet another remedy available—the *federal* writ of habeas corpus. The Supreme Court of the United States has held that a state court judgment of conviction resulting from a trial which involved a substantial error of federal constitutional dimension is void, and a prisoner held pursuant to a void judgment is unlawfully confined and subject to release by a federal court upon a writ of habeas corpus. In considering the petition for the writ a federal district judge may also order another "evidentiary hearing". And he has the power to remand the case to the state court for a new trial or for the outright release of the defendant, depending upon the kind of error committed and the evidence still available to the state.

APPEALS BY THE PROSECUTION

Only the defendant has a right to appeal the result of a trial. The constitutional protection against "double jeopardy" has been interpreted in such a way as to prevent the prosecution from appealing a case it loses.

In a growing number of jurisdictions, however, the prosecution is being accorded the right to appeal certain decisions of a pre-trial nature. The Illinois Criminal Code, for example, provides for prosecution appeals from a trial court order dismissing the charge against a defendant, or from an order suppressing a confession or other evidence alleged to have been illegally obtained.

* * *

Part II

CRIMES

Chapter 1

Crimes Against the Person

SECTION A. HOMICIDE

Homicide is the killing of one human being by another human being. Not all homicides are criminal, however. For instance, a person who kills another in self-defense has committed no crime; it is justifiable homicide. The same is true of the police officer who kills a person to prevent the commission of a forcible felony, such as robbery or burglary, when the killing is a reasonably necessary preventive measure; or when the officer kills a dangerous felon in order to prevent his escape. Then, too, some killings are excusable homicides; for instance, where a person accidentally, and without gross negligence, causes the death of another individual.

A killing amounts to a criminal homicide when it is done without lawful justification or excuse. Depending upon certain circumstances it may be either *murder* or *manslaughter*.

In the early days of our country, and prior thereto in England, the elements of the crimes of murder and manslaughter were prescribed by court decisions. These decisions came to be known as the "common law". Since then, in most jurisdictions murder and manslaughter have been redefined by the legislatures, either in the form of a separate statute or as a provision of a criminal code.

1. Murder

According to the common law, murder was the killing of a human being with "malice", and the requirement of "malice" is still found in some present-day statutes and codes. The California Penal Code, for instance, has retained it. That code provides, as did the common law, that

> ". . . malice may be express or implied. It is express when there is manifested a deliberate intention to take away the life of a fellow creature. It is implied, when no considerable provocation appears, or when the circumstances attending the killing show an abandoned and malignant heart."

A clear illustration of express malice is a case where one person intentionally pushes another off the side of a mountain. An example of implied malice is where a person fires a rifle at a moving passenger train, just "to scare" the persons aboard or to display skill at firing a bullet between the cars without hitting anyone. The dangerousness of the conduct would be evidence of "malice" as regards any killing that may be reasonably attributed to such conduct. It would indicate, to a California court or jury, "an abandoned and malignant heart".

The penalty for murder is punishable by death in some states; in others by prison terms extending to "life" or a specified number of years.

(a) Felony-Murder

Another example of a satisfaction of the element of malice is a killing during the course of a felony such as robbery. Even though a robber's gun goes off accidentally, killing the robbery victim, or a bystander, or a police officer, his conduct of committing such a dangerous crime as robbery satisfies the requirement of malice so that the killing becomes punishable as murder. A similar line of reasoning has resulted in holding co-felons guilty of murder where, in the course of an exchange of shots between robbers and the police, a police officer is accidentally killed by another officer.

Malice may also be attributed to a robber whose partner in the crime intentionally kills someone during the commission of the crime or the attempted escape. Malice on the part of all participants is implied from the dangerousness of the robbery itself; moreover, each robber is considered to act as an agent for the others in accomplishing their objective, including the attempt to escape.

This whole issue of felony-murder stems primarily from the prosecution's interest in seeking the death penalty for such killings. In some of the states which have abolished capital punishment (Wisconsin, for example), the legislatures, out of an understandable desire to punish robbers more severely whenever a killing results, have provided that the punishment for such offenses shall be fifteen years greater than that provided for non-fatal robberies.

(b) Degrees of Murder

Some states have specified varying penalties for murder, depending upon the circumstances of the killing. A "willful, deliberate and premeditated" killing, such as a poisoning or a killing during the commission of a dangerous felony, may be labeled first degree murder and punishable by death or long imprisonment. Other forms of murder may be of the second degree and punishable with a lesser penalty. According to the common law, however, there were no degrees of murder. Any unlawful killing was either murder or manslaughter.

2. Manslaughter

Manslaughter was defined at common law as an unlawful killing of another without malice. It could be either *voluntary* or *involuntary*.

Manslaughter, in contrast to murder, is usually punishable by a prison term which may range from one year to ten or fourteen years.

(a) Voluntary Manslaughter

An intentional killing upon "great provocation" *and* "in the heat of passion" constitutes the crime of voluntary manslaughter. A classic example is the killing by a husband (or wife) who unexpectedly finds his or her spouse in an act of sexual intercourse with another person, or in a situation evidencing impending or immediately concluded adulterous conduct. A killing of the paramour or of the spouse, or both, in such a circumstance would fall within the category of manslaughter because (a) the provocation was great, and (b) the killer was in the "heat of passion".

A killing of this type is treated less harshly than murder, out of consideration for the frailties of human nature. In other words, there is an understanding appreciation that the instinctive reaction of the husband (or wife) in such a situation is to kill or do other serious harm. Nevertheless, there is a feeling that such conduct should be discouraged by a criminal sanction, but one with a penalty considerably less than for the crime of murder.

It is of interest to note that in such paramour killing cases the conviction rate is quite low, primarily because of the willingness of

juries to accept occasionally the frequently concocted explanation
that the killing was done in self-defense; in other words, the paramour attacked the spouse, who killed his "attacker" only in order to
keep from being killed himself. The result of acquittal in such cases
is sometimes described in the press as an acquittal by reason of "the
unwritten law".

A few states (Texas, New Mexico, and Utah) have tried to sim-
plify the whole matter of paramour killings by legalizing such killings where the paramour is caught in the act. But in those states the
privilege does not extend to the killing of the participating spouse!

In applying the test of whether an intentional killing was upon
great provocation and in the heat of passion, the question is put to
the jury, or to the judge in non-jury cases, as to whether the accused
reacted as a "reasonable man". Technically speaking, it is not the
particular sensitivity or temper of the killer that is taken into consideration, but rather an effort is made to determine how a "reasonable
man" might have acted under similar circumstances. An illustration
of this is a famous English case where a sexually impotent man felt
insulted by the remarks of a prostitute with whom he had tried in
vain to have sexual intercourse, and he proceeded to kill her. He con-
tended that his sensitivity over his condition should be taken into
account in determining whether there was serious provocation for
this reaction, but the court held that his conduct was to be judged
by the standard of an ordinary, normal "reasonable man".

(b) Involuntary Manslaughter

Involuntary manslaughter may be described generally as an un-
intentional killing resulting from gross negligence, or as a result of
dangerous unlawful conduct. For example, a person who throws a
heavy object from the upper stories of a building into an alley used
with some frequency by pedestrians may be guilty of manslaughter
if a killing results. Likewise, a motorist may commit manslaughter if
he kills a child at a school crossing while travelling at an excessive
speed.

A number of states have created a related crime known as "reckless homicide" or "negligent homicide", for application to killings by
motorists who were driving in a reckless or grossly negligent manner. This special kind of homicide legislation was enacted because
of the difficulty encountered in convicting motorists for the more
revoltingly labeled offense of manslaughter (i.e., the slaughter of a

man), which also carried, traditionally, a *minimum* penalty of one year in the penitentiary. It was thought advisable to categorize such conduct with the less revolting label of reckless or negligent homicide and also to permit the imposition of lesser penalties than the one prescribed for manslaughter. Stated another way, it is better to obtain a reasonable number of convictions carrying relatively light penalties than to get very few convictions carrying heavy penalties. The permissible range of penalties in reckless homicide or negligent homicide statutes is generally a fine up to $1,000, or incarceration other than in a penitentiary for any period up to one year, or imprisonment in a penitentiary up to five years. (Where the traffic victim of such conduct does not die, another new statutory offense may be invoked—"reckless conduct".)

The flexibility of penalties in traffic death cases has the effect of encouraging pleas of guilty from offenders, and it results in convictions that might not be secured if a judge or jury had no choice other than a penitentiary sentence or an acquittal.

3. Federal Homicide Law

There is no general federal homicide law. There can be none, in fact, since constitutional authority is lacking for Congress to legislate upon the subject, except with respect to killings within a federal territory, in federal buildings or upon other federal property, or killings of federal officials or officers.

Example
 X, without justification or excuse, shoots and kills Y in a Post Office. X has committed a federal offense of criminal homicide.

Example
 X, a bank robber fugitive about to be apprehended by an F.B.I. agent, shoots and kills the agent. X is guilty of a federal crime of murder.

4. Modern Murder-Manslaughter Legislation

In most states the crimes of murder and manslaughter are covered in state statutes closely patterned after the common law. A trend is now under way, however, to modernize the law. The 1961 Illinois Criminal Code is a good example. In defining murder, for instance, it avoids such language as "malice" and "abandoned and malignant heart", and uses more precise and meaningful terminology.

According to the Illinois Code, a person who kills another individual *without lawful excuse* commits murder (a) if he intended to kill him or do great bodily harm; or (b) if, without intending to kill, it clearly appears that he *must have known* that his conduct probably would cause death; or (c) if death resulted from *the commission of a very serious crime* like robbery, burglary or rape.

5. Capital Punishment

For many years there has been much controversy as to whether capital punishment serves its intended purpose—a deterrent to murder. The issue is still unresolved among researchers on the subject. The capital punishment controversy has become rather academic, however, by reason of the rapid decline in executions in recent years. Although there were 199 executions in 1935, there was only one in the entire United States in 1966, two in 1967 and none in 1968. Yet in each of the latter three years over four hundred persons were under sentence of death.

In addition to an increasing unwillingness to execute murderers who have been sentenced to death, a legal concept was recently developed and enunciated by the Supreme Court of the United States regarding jury selection in capital cases that will make jury imposition of the death penalty much more difficult to obtain. The Court held that prospective jurors could not be rejected solely because of conscientious scruples against the death penalty. To do so, said the Court, constitutes a deprivation of due process, because the defendant would not then be accorded a trial by a "fair and impartial jury".

Exclusion because of such beliefs alone is permissible only when the prospective juror states that he would not consider setting them aside in the particular case for which he was called for jury service.

SECTION B. KIDNAPPING AND UNLAWFUL RESTRAINT

1. Kidnapping

The offense of kidnapping occurs when a person is unlawfully seized and secretly confined against his will.

> *Example*
>
> Mr. and Mrs. K seize Suzie, a six year old child. They take her in their car to a cottage in the country and make contact with Suzie's parents for the purpose of demanding a ransom payment. The Ks are guilty of the crime of kidnapping.

Kidnapping also occurs where an individual, by deceit, enticement, or by force or threat of force, induces another person to go from one place to another with intent to secretly confine that person against his will.

Example

Joe and Bill meet Joyce at the neighborhood bar. When the bar closes, they promise to drive Joyce home. Instead, they take her to Joe's apartment where they advise her she will be kept prisoner until she obliges them with her sexual favors. At this point, Joe and Bill have committed the offense of kidnapping.

In many jurisdictions, the confinement of a child under the age of thirteen is considered under the law to be against the will of the child regardless of any purported consent on the child's part. In many states, the penalty for kidnapping a child is greater than that for kidnapping an adult.

If the crime of kidnapping is committed while the perpetrator is masked or hooded to hide his identity, or if the victim is seriously harmed physically, a greater penalty is provided in many states. Similarly, where the kidnapping is for the purpose of obtaining a ransom or other valuable concession, some states provide for the death penalty.

Kidnapping becomes a federal crime, as well as a state crime, if the elements of the offense occur in more than one state. The constitutional basis for the federal kidnapping law covering such situations is the power of Congress to regulate "interstate commerce".

Example

Joe and Doug kidnap six-year-old Fauntleroy in State *A* and take him via State *B* to State *C* where they hold Fauntleroy pending the delivery of a ransom payment of his father. The federal kidnapping law is violated by the interstate scope of the crime. (The offense, of course, may also be prosecuted under the kidnapping law of State *A*. Moreover, technically speaking, both States *B* and *C* may have jurisdiction, respectively, to try the offense since the criminal conduct has partly occurred within those states.)

The federal kidnapping statute was enacted in 1932, shortly after the kidnapping and death of the son of the famous aviator, Charles A. Lindbergh. In 1934 it was amended to provide that after the lapse of seven days, a "presumption" arose that the kidnapped person had been taken from one state to another. The purpose of this amendment was to permit the F.B.I. to enter the investigation which otherwise would have remained exclusively a state one until events actually established a state line crossing. In 1956, following the inept handling of a kidnapping investigation by local authorities and a newspaper "leak" that resulted in the death of the kidnapped infant, the presumptive period was reduced to twenty-four hours. Consequently, the F.B.I. may now officially enter the investigation of a kidnapping case twenty-four hours after the occurrence. However, as soon as subsequent events establish that there has been no transportation of the kidnapped person outside the state the F.B.I. authority ceases; the case then becomes one within the exclusive jurisdiction of state and local police agencies.

2. Unlawful Restraint

The offense of unlawful restraint occurs when a person is detained without legal authority, even though there may have been no intent to secretly confine the victim. The penalty for unlawful restraint is less severe than that for kidnapping.

3. Detention of Suspected Shoplifters

Many states, in an effort to protect merchants from shoplifting losses, specifically provide that a merchant or an employee who reasonably believes that a person has wrongfully taken or is about to wrongfully take merchandise from the merchant's place of business may, without committing the offense of unlawful restraint, detain the suspect for a reasonable time in a reasonable manner for the purpose of ascertaining the ownership of the merchandise.

Example

Bessie Busybody, a housewife, observes Tillie Teen at the phonograph record counter of ABC Department Store. Bessie is suspicious of Tillie and thinks she saw Tillie put a record under her coat. Bessie follows Tillie to the ladies' room where she recites the "warnings" she heard the police give a suspect on her favorite TV program and refuses to let Tillie exit until she confesses to the crime. Bessie has committed the offense of unlawful restraint. However, if a saleslady had observed Tillie taking the record, she could, under some state statutes, detain Tillie for a reasonable period of time until she could determine whether or not the record was wrongfully taken.

Despite the aforementioned statutory authorization, merchants are very wary about exercising it, for fear of false arrest suits. They generally will not attempt any detention unless the person's conduct is such as to clearly warrant an actual arrest for theft. In other words, unless the person is seen taking and concealing an unpurchased article no detention is attempted. Some merchants even exercise the further precaution of delaying an arrest until the taker has left the store; in this way he is deprived of any innocent explanation for his conduct. Legally speaking, however, whenever a person's conduct evidences a probable intent to steal, a merchant, or his "store detective", is legally justified in arresting that person as a shoplifter and charging him with the crime of theft.

Section C. Battery and Assault

1. Battery

A battery occurs when a person, by any means, knowingly and unlawfully touches another person in an insulting or provoking manner. Some statutes do not require the touching to be insulting or provoking in nature so long as it was intentional and the victim has suffered bodily harm.

Example
> Joe, a student, disagreed with his college teacher's lecture and noted his dissent by spitting in the teacher's face. Joe has committed a battery.

Example
> Harry and Pete arrived in a movie house balcony at the same time from different directions. One seat was available and Harry, in order to stake claim to the seat, aggressively pushed Pete out of the way. Pete lost his balance, fell down the aisle stairway and injured himself. Harry has committed a battery.

In many jurisdictions, there is an increased penalty for the offense of battery where the offender uses a deadly weapon, or is masked or hooded in order to conceal his identity, or chooses a member of a particularly designated class of persons for his victim, such as police officers or teachers. Also, where the offender, in committing a battery, causes permanent disability or disfigurement to his victim, a more serious penalty is provided, under the title of an offense known as "mayhem".

2. Assault

An assault occurs when a person, without lawful authority, does something that places another person in reasonable apprehension of receiving a battery.

An assault does not involve a touching. If a touching occurs, the offense is a battery.

Example

Jim, a husky six-footer, got into an argument at a party with another guest, jockey-sized Ron. Jim took a punch at Ron, but because of his myopia (of which Ron was not aware) missed by a foot. Other guests restrained Jim from any further action. Jim is guilty of assault. Had he connected, it would have been a battery.

Example

Joe, enraged at Bill, backed him against a wall and fired a loaded pistol at him. The pistol jammed and did not fire. Joe is guilty of attempted murder, as discussed in another section of this book. But he is also guilty of assault in that he put Bill in reasonable apprehension of receiving a battery.

As in the case of battery, an assault occurring while the offender is masked or hooded, or which is performed with use of a deadly weapon, or which is performed against a member of a particular class of persons (designated by the legislature), often calls for a greater penalty than simple assault. (See above example.)

SECTION D. SEX OFFENSES AND RELATED CRIMINAL CONDUCT

1. Forcible Rape

The crime of rape was originally defined as the unlawful sexual intercourse with a female "by force and against her will". Although many of the early cases held that a woman was required to resist "to the utmost", a submission out of fear of violence is now generally held to be rape.

An early statute in England declared that intercourse with a child under ten years of age was also rape, regardless of "consent".

What about the case where a woman is so drunk as to be utterly incapable of consenting? In such a situation the act is presumed to be without her consent and therefore rape. Modern statutes generally provide that rape is committed whenever the woman is unconscious (from drink, drugs, etc.), or is so mentally deranged or deficient that she cannot give effective consent to the act of intercourse.

Since the crime of rape requires that the sexual act be unlawful, a married man could not be guilty of "raping" his wife. Marriage rendered the act "lawful". It is of interest to note, however, that if a married man compelled his wife to have intercourse with another man, the husband could be found guilty of rape. His conduct renders him an "accessory" to the rape (as subsequently discussed in Chapter 6) and therefore guilty of the crime itself. Under a similar line of reasoning, a *woman* might be convicted of raping another woman.

Intercourse, within the meaning of the crime of rape, consists of any penetration, however slight, of the female sex organ by the male sex organ. An emission is not required for the crime.

2. Sex Offenses Against Children

(a) Statutory Rape

In an effort to protect the young from sexual conduct with older persons, various legislatures have created separate sex offenses applicable to such situations. One is the crime of "statutory rape"—sexual intercourse with a female under a certain age, usually 16, regardless of whether or not she consents. A mistaken belief that the girl was over the specified age has been generally held not to be a defense, regardless of the reasonableness of the belief, although there are a few decisions and statutory provisions to the contrary.

(b) Indecent Liberties and Contributing to Sexual Delinquency

Modern legislation, in an effort to further protect the young, has established several additional offenses. One is "indecent liberties with a child"; another is "contributing to the sexual delinquency of a child". The two offenses consist essentially of any lewd fondling for the purpose of arousing the sexual desires of either the male or the female under the specified age (e.g. under 16).

(c) Incest

Another offense, also intended primarily for protection of the young, is "incest". The classic example is sexual intercourse by a father with his daughter. However, the offense has been extended to include mothers and sons, and brothers and sisters (and, in some states, other blood relatives too). In such situations consent is no defense.

3. Adultery and Fornication

Adultery is the act of sexual intercourse between one married person and another person other than his or her spouse. For divorce purposes one "sneak" experience is sufficient, but in most jurisdictions, for the act to constitute a crime the parties must engage in such conduct under circumstances whereby their behavior is well known to others. To use the favorite statutory language, the adulterous conduct must be "open and notorious".

The lesser offense of "fornication" generally consists of cohabitation or sexual intercourse between unmarried persons under circumstances whereby their behavior is well known to others; in other words, "open and notorious".

In some states, Louisiana being one, there is no such crime as adultery or fornication. This is also generally true in foreign countries.

4. Bigamy

A person who has a husband or wife and marries another commits the crime of bigamy. In some states a defense to the charge of bigamy is that the accused reasonably believed the prior marriage had been legally dissolved or that the prior spouse was dead.

5. Deviate Sexual Conduct

In years past, a rather universal rule prevailed in this country that made criminal practically any sexual gratification derived from male and female intimacies other than the one with the potential of reproduction. Any oral-genital contact, even between husband and wife in the privacy of their home, was unlawful. So was any sexual activity between members of the same sex. And, most certainly, any human-animal sexual contact was prohibited and severely punishable.

The trend in recent years is to remove the stigma of criminality from all forms of sexual conduct carried on in privacy between adult males and females. Homosexuality, for instance, has been removed from the list of crimes in at least one state, but only when the conduct is consensual, is committed in private, and does not involve a young person with an older one.

6. Prostitution and Related Offenses

Prostitution was not a common law crime, although keeping a house of prostitution was. The keeping of the so-called "bawdy house" was considered to be corruptive of public morals, whereas the act of prostitution itself was not viewed so seriously. Today, however, both kinds of conduct are generally unlawful.

Some states have also made it an offense to solicit or to patronize a prostitute. Outlawed, too, are certain kinds of related conduct involving a third party, in addition to the prostitute and her patron, such as "solicitation for a prostitute", "pandering" or "pimping". These are types of offenses that commonly involve "organized crime" and are labeled "commercialized vice".

7. The Federal "White Slave" (Mann) Act

A federal statute, passed by Congress in 1910, but amended to some extent thereafter, makes it a crime "to knowingly transport in interstate or foreign commerce, or in the District of Columbia or in any Territory or Possession of the United States, any woman or girl for the purpose of prostitution or debauchery, or for any other immoral purpose, or with the intent and purpose to induce, entice, or compel her to become a prostitute or to give herself up to debauchery, or to engage in any other immoral practice".

This Act of Congress, known as the White Slave Act, or as the Mann Act (because it had been introduced as a bill by Representative James R. Mann), was intended to discourage the "commercial vice" of traffic in women for monetary gain. It has been interpreted, however, to cover the transportation of a woman across state lines to become the concubine or mistress of the transporter; in other words, the transportation need not be for monetary gain. All that is required is transportation for an "immoral purpose" or an "immoral practice", whatever those terms may be interpreted to mean in any given case situation. In actuality, however, the act is rarely used except in cases of commercialized vice.

8. Public Annoyance by Sexual Indecency
   ## or by Other Sexually Motivated Conduct

(a) Exhibitionism

According to common law, any "obscene" or "indecent" act of a public nature was a crime, by reason of its injurious effect upon "public morality". Under this basic principle it was a punishable offense for a person to "indecently" expose his sexual organs in public, which act of exhibitionism is usually committed for the purpose of sexual gratification to the exhibitor. Today such conduct is made criminal by a specific ordinance or statute. In the alternative, prosecutions are brought under some general statute such as "disorderly conduct", defined in certain legislative enactments as any act done in such an unreasonable manner as to alarm or disturb another person *and* to provoke a breach of the peace. (The offense of "disorderly conduct" is discussed in a subsequent section of this book.)

(b) Window Peeping

Prosecutions were attempted against "window peepers" or "peeping Toms" under the common law concept of acts affecting "public morality", but the courts were reluctant to classify such conduct within that category. On the other hand, considerable difficulty has been encountered whenever attempts have been made to draft legislation dealing specifically with conduct of that nature. Constitutional "due process" guarantees against legislative "vagueness" or "indefiniteness" have presented problems of an almost unsurmountable nature.

If the window peeping were done in such a way as to provoke a "breach of the peace", disorderly conduct might be involved, but ordinarily a window peeper indulges in his conduct in secrecy and darkness.

About as close as legislative draftsmen can come is to make it an offense to enter upon the property of another and to look into a dwelling for a "lewd and unlawful purpose". But here again, it is difficult to prove that purpose. In any event, the individual who enters upon the property of another without authority might be subject to another and more easily established offense—trespass.

(c) Anonymous Telephone Calls

One of the most annoying, though generally harmless, acts of misconduct is the anonymous telephone call that is usually motivated by sexual gratification. The caller may do no more than telephone a woman for the purpose of just hearing her voice, without saying anything himself, or he may use obscene language, or he may make indecent proposals to her.

The problem of the anonymous telephone caller is usually dealt with in the state statutes governing the general use of telephones, rather than in the criminal laws. They prohibit, among other things, the use over the telephone of language that is "obscene, lewd or immoral, with the intent to offend another person". A federal statute also makes it an offense to use the telephone in that manner.

Chapter 2

Crimes Against Property

SECTION A. THEFT AND RELATED OFFENSES

1. Larceny

The earliest common law crime aimed at discouraging what laymen usually refer to as theft was larceny. It consisted of the *taking* and *carrying away* of *personal property* of another, with *intent to steal* (i.e., "permanently deprive" another of his property). If any one of these elements was missing in a particular case the accused could not be found guilty of larceny.

One of the early difficulties in larceny prosecutions occurred where the owner of the property had relinquished possession to another person who thereafter converted it to his own use, or otherwise disposed of it. For instance, if X asked Y to lend him his horse to go to town and on the way X sold the horse, there could be no larceny because the element of "taking" was not present.

2. Larceny by Bailee, and Embezzlement

In an effort to "plug up the loophole" in the crime of larceny, so as to get to the person who converts personal property to his own use *after having received possession* of it from the owner, the English Parliament and early American legislatures created the new crimes of "larceny by bailee" and "embezzlement".

> *Example*
> X is given a package of merchandise to deliver to Y. X, considered the "bailee", sells it to Z. X has committed "larceny by bailee".

32

Example
    X, a bank teller, pockets $500.00 which he received for deposit. He has committed the crime of embezzlement.

3. False Pretenses and Confidence Games

Another early effort to take care of deficiency in the original definition of the offense of larceny was the creation of the offense of obtaining money or property under "false pretenses" or by means of a "confidence game". The former was usually a misdemeanor while the latter was usually a felony.

4. Modern Theft Legislation

Modern legislation is fast doing away with the various theft crimes that have had a variety of labels in times past, and which created troublesome problems of interpretation.

An example of this is the 1961 Illinois Criminal Code. Formerly there were seventy-four separate statutory provisions in Illinois dealing with the problem of theft. Most of them were enacted over a period of many years for the purpose of plugging up loopholes in preceding statutes; now there is basically one provision under the title "theft" that covers practically all of the situations which were the basis for the multitude of earlier enactments, including the crime of "receiving stolen property". The Illinois Code simply provides that a person commits the crime of theft when he (a) *knowingly* obtains or exerts unauthorized control over another person's property, or obtains control by deception or threats, or (b) receives stolen property (or receives such property under circumstances which would reasonably indicate it was stolen), *and* when he also intended to deprive the owner permanently of the use or benefit of the property.

The punishment for a theft of the common law larceny variety was usually of two grades, based upon the monetary value of the object taken. For instance, if it were under $15 the offense was labeled as "petit larceny"; if over that amount it was termed "grand larceny". "Petit larceny" was considered a misdemeanor, punishable by a jail sentence up to one year. "Grand larceny" was considered a felony, punishable by a penitentiary sentence of a year or more. Today, the dividing line between petit larceny and grand larceny is usually set at a larger amount, such as $100 or $150, thereby reflecting the monetary inflation of current times.

Another variance with regard to punishment occurred when the theft was from the person of another, but without his knowledge; for example, the act of pickpocketting. In such instances, in deference to the physical danger to the victim, the statutory penalty is generally more severe than a stealing other than from the person.

5. Robbery

Robbery is generally defined as the taking of money or personal property from the person of another by force or threat of force.

> *Example*
> X grabs Y around the neck and removes his wallet; or X, at gunpoint, demands and receives Y's wallet.

6. Burglary

Burglary at common law consisted of the *breaking and entering* of the *dwelling house* of another, *in the nighttime,* with *intent to steal.*

Many of the early cases involved such questions as what constitutes "a breaking". Suppose a door was slightly ajar and the would-be thief merely shoved it far enough to squeeze his body through? Suppose he hid in a trunk that was labeled for delivery into a home and thereby effected an entry?

The meaning of "dwelling house" also presented a problem. Suppose the building was a summer home or cottage and the breaking and entry occurred in the winter time when it was unoccupied and boarded up? Even the meaning of "nighttime" caused some trouble, where the act occurred near the twilight period.

These various and troublesome problems are being gradually resolved by legislative enactments which simply state that a person commits burglary when, without authority, he knowingly enters, or without authority remains within, a building, housetrailer, watercraft, aircraft, railroad car, or any part thereof, with intent to commit therein a felony or theft. Such legislation eliminates any controversy as to "breaking and entering", "dwelling house", or "nighttime".

Always, however, there remains the difficulty of establishing in all cases the element of "intent", but this has, and will continue to be, a problem, as long as we adhere to the fundamentally desirable concept that no one should be punished for such a serious offense as burglary unless he *intended* to do a wrong. Otherwise a person who enters a building or other structures by mistake could suffer the consequences of being convicted of burglary.

Because of the danger it poses to life and limb, burglary, along with robbery, is punishable more severely than a theft under non-dangerous circumstances.

7. Forgery

Forgery occurs when a person knowingly makes, alters, issues, delivers or possesses with intent to issue or deliver any document capable of and designed to defraud another person.

Example
John wrote a check payable to himself and signed it with a fictitious name. He endorsed the check and cashed it at the local tavern. John is guilty of forgery.

Example
Bill owed Pete $100.00 and sent him a $10.00 check in partial payment. Pete knew Bill had "plenty" in the bank so he added an extra zero and changed the amount to $100.00 before cashing it. Pete is guilty of forgery.

Example
Harry is planning a business trip abroad. His friend Tom, a bank official, issues a letter of credit from his bank stating that Harry has $100,000.00 credit with the bank, when in fact he has no such credit. Harry carries this letter with him to use in case he comes across a favorable business deal requiring a showing of his financial responsibilities. Both Harry and Tom are guilty of forgery.

The forging of legal tender (money) is a federal offense and is called "counterfeiting".

8. Interstate Transportation of Stolen Property, and the Theft of Property in Interstate Shipment

Several federal statutes prohibit and prescribe punishment for the interstate transportation of stolen property, or for the theft of property being transported from one state to another. The authorization for federal legislation of this type is derived from the constitutional power of Congress to regulate interstate commerce.

Example
X steals an automobile in State A and drives it into State B. X, in addition to committing the state offense of theft, has committed a federal crime.

Example

> A television manufacturer in State A ships by truck or rail a number of television sets to a dealer in State B. On the way X and Y remove and make off with several of the sets, or perhaps even the entire shipment. They have committed a federal offense.

An interstate theft of property is also punishable in the court of the state in which it occurred. Ordinarily, however, the charge is brought and tried in the federal courts alone.

9. Thefts and Theft Related Offenses Involving Federal Property or National Banks and Federally Insured Organizations Generally

A theft of property belonging to the United States Government may be punished by the state within which it occurs, as well as by the federal government itself. In such instances, however, the state authorities relinquish their own right to prosecute. The same procedure usually prevails with regard to embezzlements from national banks and other federally insured corporations and organizations, and also in the case of burglaries and robberies committed within such institutions.

√ 10. "Misprision of Felony" and "Compounding a Crime"

Under the subject of theft it is highly appropriate to discuss the little known, yet very important offense known as "misprision of felony" or "compounding a crime". The nature of this offense may best be described by quoting from both a federal statute and a state statute upon the subject.

The federal statute provides as follows:

> *Misprision of Felony:* Whoever, having knowledge of the actual commission of a felony, [an offense punishable under federal law by a term of more than one year], conceals and does not as soon as possible make known the same to some judge or other person in civil or military authority under the United States, shall be fined not more than $500 or imprisoned not more than three years, or both.

Example

> X knows that Y has stolen property, over $100 in value, from a post office, or from a Navy shipyard. If X fails to report the matter he is guilty of misprision of felony.

Example

A, a bank president, knows that B, a teller in a national bank, has embezzled over $100. If A does not report it he commits misprision of felony.

The states have not been so demanding as the federal government with regard to a person who only has knowledge that another person has committed a felony. Unless the person with such knowledge does something affirmatively to cover up the crime, or to assist the felon to escape, etc., he does not violate a state law. About as far as the states have been willing to go is to create the crime of "compounding a crime".

The statutory offense of "compounding a crime" is sometimes phrased as follows: "A person compounds a crime when he receives or offers to another any consideration for a promise not to prosecute or aid in the prosecution of an offender."

Example

Employee X steals or embezzles $5000 from Employer Y. X's father offers $1000 in restitution, upon Y's promise not to initiate a prosecution against X. X's father is guilty of "compounding a crime" by reason of his offer, and if Y accepts the restitution money he, too, is guilty of that offense.

It should be pointed out, however, that after a prosecution has been initiated a court may withhold punishment upon a guilty plea in instances where the thief or someone on his behalf agrees to make, and does make, some restitution satisfactory to the victim.

SECTION B. PROPERTY DAMAGE AND INTRUSIONS UPON PROPERTY

1. Arson

Of all the acts directed at damage to property, the most serious is the crime of arson. A good modern definition of arson is the following, in statutory form:

A person commits arson when, by fire or explosive, he knowingly:
  (a) Damages any real property, or any personal property having a value of $150.00 or more, of another person without his consent; or
  (b) With intent to defraud an insurer, damages any property or any personal property having a value of $150.00 or more.

Property "of another" means a building or other property, whether real or personal, in which a person other than the offender has an interest which the offender has no authority to defeat or impair, even though the offender may also have an interest in the building or property.

The foregoing provision avoids the uncertainties in the old, common law definition of arson. For instance, there need no longer be any quibbling as to whether a "burning" had occurred; it is sufficient that there has been "damage" caused by fire or explosive.

The provision also covers the burning of one's own property, where the purpose is to defraud an insurer. At common law the property had to be another person's dwelling house.

The figure of $150.00, whether in connection with one's own property, or the personal property of someone else, has no particular magic; it could be set at $100.00 or at $300.00, or at any other figure a legislature might desire. This monetary specification is only intended to draw the line between felony and misdemeanor. As will be seen in the next section, a damage to another person's personal property (i.e., not real estate) of lesser value is also punishable, but only as the misdemeanor of "criminal damage to property".

The penalty for arson is generally a very severe one. Moreover, if death occurs because of this inherently dangerous offense of arson —or, rather, if the death can be considered a reasonably foreseeable result of the act and the circumstances surrounding it—the offender is guilty of felony-murder.

2. Other Intentional Damage to Property

As previously stated, criminal damage to property by fire or explosive constitutes the felony of arson, whenever a legislature has seen fit to label it as such. Other kinds of intentional damage to another person's property are also punishable criminally, but less severely than arson. Moreover, even when fire or an explosive is used to damage personal property, that is, not a building, the penalty for the conduct may be placed in the misdemeanor category if the value of the property is under the specified amount.

The offense of criminal damage to personal property may also include injuries to domestic animals.

Some legislatures have described lesser forms of the foregoing kind of damage to property as "malicious mischief".

3. Trespass

A person who enters upon the land of another, after receiving, immediately prior to such entry, notice from the owner or occupant that such entry is forbidden commits the offense of trespass. A trespass is also committed whenever a person remains upon the land of another after receiving notice to depart.

The required notice may be oral or in writing. If in writing, it must be conspicuously posted or exhibited, and particularly at the main entrance or at points where access seems available.

Chapter 3

Offenses Affecting Public Morals, Health, Safety, and Welfare

The First Amendment to the Constitution of the United States sets out the guarantees of freedom of speech and freedom of the press. However, those freedoms have been held by the courts not to include the protection of obscenity; and because obscenity is not constitutionally protected, it is a crime to sell, publish, disseminate, or possess with intent to disseminate, an obscene picture or writing. Similarly, it is a crime to perform, direct, produce or promote an obscene act or performance. However, the Supreme Court has recently held that it is no crime to possess obscene material in the privacy of one's home.

Criminal prosecutions under the obscenity laws have been conducted in cases involving photographs, magazines, books, movies and theatrical performances.

1. The Guidelines for Determining Obscenity

To determine whether a particular picture, writing or performance is obscene, the following test must be applied:

(1) Does the dominant theme to the material, taken as a whole, appeal to a morbid or shameful ("prurient") interest in nudity, sex or excretion?

(2) In determining the dominant theme of the material in accordance with point (1), the material must be examined through the viewpoint of an "average person", based upon "contemporary community standards".

40

(3) "Contemporary community" standards, as used in point (2), generally means national standards of acceptance of this type of material; is the material "patently offensive"?

(4) If the material is objectionable under the guidelines of points (1), (2), and (3), then the court must inquire whether it is utterly without any redeeming social, literary, historical, scientific or other value.

In cases where the question as to whether or not there is any redeeming importance is a close one, the method of advertising or exploiting the material may be examined. Thus, if the material is exploited or advertised to stress the lewd or lascivious aspects of the material, it will be considered without redeeming importance. However, if the advertising or exploiting of the material stresses the purported redeeming nature of the material it might be considered as being of redeeming social importance and, therefore, not obscene.

The following factual examples illustrate the application of the above four guidelines for testing obscenity:

Example

A motion picture used for the training of gynecologists is seized by the police. This film contains numerous scenes of nude women. This film is not obscene. Although it appeals to an interest in sex or nudity, the interest is neither shameful nor morbid.

Example

A local bookstore is selling an 18th century English novel detailing the affairs of a nymphomaniac. This book may not be obscene. Although the primary interest of the book is a morbid interest in sex, it may contain redeeming historical or literary merit. The book may be well-written and it may accurately elucidate the morality of a segment of society in an historical period of England.

Example

The police seize a photograph from a youth in which a man and woman are portrayed in the nude in an act of sexual intercourse. This photograph is considered obscene. It appeals to a morbid or shameful interest in sex and nudity. There is no redeeming merit.

In order to convict a person of the offense of obscenity, it must be shown that he knew the nature of the obscene material. Showing this knowledge is called proof of "scienter". "Scienter" is rarely proved directly, that is, by an admission of the person charged that he knew the nature of the obscene material. Most often "scienter" is shown circumstantially from the facts involved in the case. The following factual examples show an existence of "scienter":

Example

A book seller has a substantial stock of obscene books kept in a separate section of his store. These books were supplied by a wholesale firm which deals exclusively in obscene books. The bookseller had visited this wholesale firm on many occasions and purchased similar books there upon those occasions. Such circumstances establish his knowledge that the books were obscene.

Example

Defendant was "the managing partner of an enterprise that specialized in books of a salacious character". He prepared the newspaper advertising for the books. He admitted that he knew they could not be sent through the mails because of their character. Proof of knowledge of the obscene nature of the books is thereby established.

Example

The books in question were printed on cheap paper and contained obscene cover pictures. They were also priced very high and an excessive profit resulted. Knowledge of the obscene character of the books is thereby established.

Example

The sales prices of the small paperback books were $4.50 each. The books were kept by defendant next to the cash register. The covers of the books were "themselves obscene and offensive". The covers of the books also bore the warning "Adults Only". Here, too, the required element of knowledge is present.

The legal procedures for determining whether a motion picture is obscene differ from those relating to books and art.

Motion pictures may be subject to "prior restraint" (censorship) as a condition to being licensed for showing. Material other than motion pictures may not be subject to pre-release censorship, or "prior restraint"; an arrest for obscenity may be made only *after* the publication or performance of the alleged obscene material. On the other hand, pre-release censorship, or "prior restraint", may be exercised with respect to motion pictures. This principle has been approved by the United States Supreme Court.

A governmental body, therefore, may require "submission of motion pictures in advance of exhibition", but the Supreme Court has stated prior restraint procedures must be accompanied by certain safeguards, such as the following:

(1) The burden of proving a film obscene rests upon the governmental agency.

(2) The government may not make a final determination that a film is obscene without court approval of that determination. This is done by the government obtaining an injunction against the showing of the film.

(3) Both the government's administrative procedures and the court's judicial procedures must allow for a speedy final determination as to whether or not the showing of the film may be prohibited on the ground of obscenity.

Where a motion picture is licensed by a government board, the motion picture, its distributor and exhibitor are protected from prosecution under the criminal law for obscenity and the police department may not make an arrest based on its independent judgment that the motion picture is obscene.

Following the suggestion of some of the members of the United States Supreme Court, a few jurisdictions have abandoned full censorship of films in favor of a limited form of "prior restraint", often referred to as "classification" of films. Under a "classification" procedure, only those films which are to be shown to audiences which include children must be licensed. The procedural safeguard requirements are the same as for full censorship.

2. Practical Inhibitions in the Enforcement of Obscenity Laws

The police and the prosecution are often indiscriminately and unfairly criticized for permitting the sale of "filthy" books and the exhibition of "dirty" films.

As a practical matter, there is little that law enforcement can do with respect to borderline offensive films and literature. The United States Supreme Court's definition of obscenity excludes materials which have the "slightest" amount of "redeeming social, literary, historical or esthetic value", no matter how prurient its over-all appeal may be. Thus, if 90% (or perhaps even 99%) of the appeal is to a "prurient" interest, the courts would not classify the book or film to be obscene if the other 10% (or perhaps even 1%) of appeal was to a social, historical, etc. interest. How then can a beautifully filmed and artistically directed pornographic movie ever be obscene? And how can a magazine full of suggestive nudity be obscene when it includes a quality article on photography or human anatomy?

The Supreme Court has also laid down costly and difficult procedural requirements for the censorship of films, which inhibits most states and municipalities from taking any legal action. Also, the court has set forth special requirements for the issuance and execution of search warrants for obscene material, which makes it more difficult to seize such materials than any other contraband.

The public, frustrated by what it considers police-prosecution inaction or indifference, is for the most part not aware of the technical prohibitions placed upon law enforcement officers. If the basic responsibility for the present situation is to be placed upon any branch of government, it must rest upon the judiciary rather than the police and prosecution.

SECTION B. ABORTION

An illegal abortion occurs when a person, without legal justification, uses any instrument, or administers any medicine, drug or other substance with the intent to cause a rejection or removal of the fetus from a pregnant woman. It is punishable as a felony. An attempt to commit such an act is also a felony. If death results, the offense escalates to felony-murder.

In most states, the only legal justification for an abortion is the preservation of the *life* of the pregnant woman. A few jurisdictions, however, permit abortions to be performed when necessary to preserve the *health* of the pregnant woman. The District of Columbia is an example of the latter.

Within the past several years, a few states (e.g., Colorado, North Carolina) have enacted statutes which legalize abortions when performed by a physician in a licensed hospital for the following additional reasons:

> (1) When medically advisable because the fetus would be born with a grave and irremediable physical or mental defect; or
> (2) The pregnancy is the result of a forcible rape or incest.

Example

A pregnant woman receives medication (e.g., Thalidomide) to relieve her discomfort, but the medical profession subsequently ascertains that a frequent "side effect" of the medication is the production of horrible physical deformities in the child (e.g., no limbs). An abortion would be permissible.

Example

A girl is physically forced, or threatened with force, to submit to sexual intercourse with her father, and she becomes pregnant. An abortion would be permissible.

In most jurisdictions, a person can be convicted of an attempted abortion even though the woman was not in fact pregnant.

Example

Milly woke up one morning with a stomach ache. She decided she was pregnant and told her boy friend so. The two of them went to a one-time physician who previously had lost his license for performing an illegal abortion. He inserted a surgical device in her vagina, withdrew it and announced that the abortion was successful. On learning of the foregoing, Milly's parents reported the incident to the police. In most jurisdictions, the doctor would be guilty of attempted illegal abortion. The fact that Milly was not pregnant would be no defense to the charges.

Under the wording of some state statutes the distinction between abortion and attempted abortion has been abolished. The crime of abortion covers both. Moreover, the same statute may settle the foregoing case situation where the woman actually was not pregnant. Such a statute may read as follows:

A person commits abortion when he uses any instrument, drug or other substance, with the intent to procure a miscarriage of any woman. It shall not be necessary in order to commit abortion that such woman be pregnant, or if pregnant, that a miscarriage be in fact accomplished.

Section C. Gambling

There are many different types of conduct which constitute the offense of gambling, the most common of which are the following:

1. Wagering by Participant

The offense of gambling occurs when a person plays a game of chance or skill for money or other things of value.

Example

Several men play poker for stakes of $1.00 limit every Friday night at a local men's club. Their conduct constitutes unlawful gambling. However, where it is a simple social event, not involving profit to a sponsoring individual or to the club itself, rarely is there any police interference.

Many states provide for an exemption to their gambling laws for the awarding of prizes or compensation to the actual contestants in a bona fide contest for the determination of skill, speed, strength or endurance.

Example

A country club stages a professional golf tournament. The winner is to receive $10,000.00. Other professional golfers who finish high in the tournament standings are to receive lesser compensations. This is not a gambling activity.

2. Wagering by Bystander

The offense of gambling occurs when a person makes a wager upon any game, contest, or other occurrence involving persons other than himself.

Example

Phil and Joe and their friends sit in the right field bleachers at the local ball park and bet on various aspects of the baseball game, that is, whether the next pitch will be a ball or a strike, whether the batter will get on base, whether the pitcher will complete the game, etc. This is unlawful gambling activity.

Exempted from the foregoing prohibition against bystander gambling are insurance agreements to compensate for losses due to fire, storms, death, etc.

Another usual exemption is the awarding of prizes or compensation to owners of animals or vehicles that are entered in a bona fide contest for the determination of skill, speed, strength, or endurance.

By a considerable stretch of judicial reasoning, pari-mutuel race track betting has been held valid even in states whose Constitutions contain prohibitions against gambling.

3. Possession of Gambling Devices

A gambling offense occurs in most states when a person operates, keeps, owns, uses, purchases, exhibits, rents, sells, bargains for the sale or lease of, manufactures, or distributes any gambling device. A common statutory definition of a "gambling device" is: any clock, tape machine, slot machine, or other machine or device for the reception of money or other thing of value on chance or skill or upon the action of which money or other thing of value is staked, hazarded, bet, won or lost; or any mechanism, furniture, fixture, equipment or other device designed primarily for use in a gambling place. A "gambling device" does not ordinarily include:

(1) a coin-in-the-slot-operated mechanical device played for amusement which rewards the player with the right to replay such mechanical device, which device is so constructed or devised as to make the result of the operation thereof depend in part upon the skill of the player, and which returns to the player thereof no money, property or right to receive money or property.

(2) Vending machines by which full and adequate return is made for the money invested and in which there is no element of chance or hazard.

Example

A country club has several slot machines. The proceeds from these machines are used to purchase gifts for veterans at the local V.A. Hospital. However worthy the cause may be, the machines are gambling devices, prohibited by law.

Example

A country club has a mechanical bowling machine and a candy bar vending machine (which sometimes inadvertently gives two candy bars for the price of one). These machines are not gambling devices.

4. Bookmaking

The offense of gambling occurs when a person owns or possesses any book, instrument or apparatus by means of which bets or wagers have been, or are, recorded or registered, or knowingly possesses any money which he has received in the course of a bet or wager. This activity is commonly called "bookmaking".

Example

Sam, the proprietor of Sam's Cigar Store, takes wagers at his store for the "syndicate." Sam records these wagers in a ledger. Sam is guilty of gambling.

5. Poolselling

The offense of gambling occurs when a person sells pools upon the result of any game or contest of skill or chance, political nomination, appointment, or election.

Example

Ten or more members of the steno pool at an office each contribute $1.00 to the Kentucky Derby "pot". Each girl draws a slip of paper from a bowl containing the names of all the horses entered in the race. The girl who has the slip with the name of the winning horse wins the money in the pot. All the girls have committed the offense of gambling. This infraction of the law, however, is rarely prosecuted.

6. Lottery (Raffle)

The offense of gambling (unlawful lottery) occurs when a person sets up or promotes any lottery or sells, offers to sell or transfers any ticket or share for any lottery. A "lottery" is any scheme or procedure whereby one or more prizes are distributed by chance among persons who have paid or promised consideration for a chance to win such prizes, and regardless of whether the scheme or procedure is a raffle, gift, sale, or by some other name. Supermarket promotional games are usually exempted by statute or case decision from the definition of an unlawful lottery, on the theory that a purchase of goods is not required in order for a person to obtain a chance or ticket.

Example

The local church runs a "bingo" game where bingo cards are sold for $1.00 each per game. Valuable prizes are awarded for the winner. The profits from the game go for missionary and other charitable work. This is unlawful gambling activity in most states.

Example

The local supermarket gives a stamp containing a picture of a baseball player to each customer or other person who comes in the store and asks for one. When a customer collects five bearing the pictures of five different players he receives $100 in cash. In most jurisdictions, this would not be an unlawful lottery.

7. "Numbers", "Policy", and "Bolita"

"Numbers", "policy", and "bolita", like lottery, are illegal in that they involve the payment of a sum of money for the chance to win a greater sum of money.

Example

Bill sells tickets containing four numbers each for the "Wheel of Fortune" game. After the tickets are sold, Bill spins his roulette-type wheel four times. The holder of the ticket containing the four numbers selected by the wheel is awarded one-half of the total funds collected by Bill from the sale of the tickets. This is an unlawful gambling activity.

8. Keeping a Gambling Place

The offense of keeping a gambling place occurs when a person knowingly permits any premises or property owned or occupied by him or under his control to be used as a gambling place. A common statutory definition of a gambling place includes any real estate, vehicle, boat or any other property whatsoever used for the purpose of gambling.

Some states, in addition to penalizing a keeper of a gambling place, provide that the gambling place may be proceeded against as a "nuisance" under state law. If declared by a court to be a nuisance, the building where the gambling occurred may be "padlocked" for a period of time, perhaps for as long as a year.

Some states provide for the forfeiture of a liquor license of a tavern where gambling occurs, and also for the court sale of a gambling place to pay any unsatisfied fine.

9. Syndicated Gambling

In a special effort to suppress gambling that is controlled by organized crime syndicates, a few states have enacted "syndicated gambling" laws which prescribe a considerably greater penalty whenever the nature of the gambling clearly indicates a large scale operation. This may be based upon the size of the bets, the number of bets, and other factors.

10. Miscellaneous Gambling Laws

Most jurisdictions have statutory provisions which provide for the forfeiture of gambling devices and gambling funds confiscated in a lawful search and seizure. The gambling funds so seized are usually authorized by statute to be forfeited to the state, county or municipality treasury and the gambling devices so seized are usually authorized to be destroyed by the local law enforcement authorities.

Example
> Pursuant to a proper search warrant, the police raid the back room of Joe's Cigar Store. A poker game is in progress and two slot machines are being played. After Joe's conviction for being the keeper of a gambling place, the money used in the poker game and in the slot machines is forfeited to the County treasury, and the machines destroyed.

Gambling agreements are not enforceable by court proceeding since they are considered "contracts contrary to public policy".

Example
> Sam placed a bet with Bill, a bookmaker, on a football game. Sam cannot sue Bill for any money due him.

11. Federal Prohibitions

As a result of the shocking disclosures in 1950 during the course of the hearings conducted by a Special Senate Committee to Investigate Organized Crime in Interstate Commerce, under the Chairmanship of the late Senator Estes Kefauver, Congress began to consider various ways and means whereby effective congressional assistance could be given to the states in an attempt to suppress illegal gambling. The first development, in 1959, was the enactment of a statute prohibiting the interstate transportation of gambling devices. This was done in the exercise of the power of Congress to regulate interstate commerce. And upon the same authorization Congress subsequently prohibited the interstate transportation of wagering "paraphernalia" and wagering "information".

SECTION D. POSSESSION AND SALE OF NARCOTIC DRUGS

Most states define narcotics in a manner similar to the federal law definition. Narcotic drugs are usually defined to include opium, isonipecaine, and coca leaves, whether produced directly or indirectly by extraction from substances of vegetable origin, or independently by means of chemical synthesis, or by a combination of extraction and chemical synthesis. Narcotics drugs include any compound of opium, isonipecaine and coca leaves. Also included are any other substances which are chemically identical with these drugs.

Of the more frequently used narcotic drugs, morphine, codeine, and heroin are derivatives of opium. Cocaine is derived from coca leaves.

Although not a narcotic drug in the scientific sense, for the purposes of criminal law, marijuana (all parts of the plant Cannabis sativa) is treated as one. Also, most jurisdictions now treat hallucinogenic drugs, such as LSD (lysergic acid and related compounds), the same as narcotic drugs under the law. The same is true of methedrine ("speed").

1. State Laws

Most states have laws which prohibit the manufacture, sale, purchase, possession, or dispensing of narcotic drugs.

Example

Paul gives Louise, a high school student, a marijuana cigarette. She accepts it. Both Paul and Louise have violated the law, although Paul would probably be subjected to the greater penalty. Moreover, as a practical matter, Louise would probably not be prosecuted if she agreed to testify against Paul.

Example

Joe sells heroin to Tom, Dick and Harry, who in turn sell the drugs to persons at twice the price they paid for it. Joe, the wholesaler, Tom, Dick and Harry, the retailers, have all violated the law. Again, since Joe is the more serious offender, as a practical matter, the prosecution would probably treat the retailers more leniently if they cooperated in the prosecution of Joe.

Example

Jim and Frank, high school students, discreetly manufacture LSD in the high school chemistry lab and distribute the drug to fellow students. In many states *all* the students would have violated the law.

2. Federal Laws

Congress has made it "unlawful to import or bring any narcotic drug into the United States"; and "whoever . . . receives, conceals,

buys, sells, or in any manner facilitates the transportation, concealment, or sale of any such narcotic drug after being brought in,
knowing the same to have been imported or brought into the United
States contrary to law, or conspires to commit any of such acts . . ."
also commits a federal offense. The penalty is five to twenty years
imprisonment and, in addition, a fine of not more than $20,000. A
subsequent offense calls for ten to forty years imprisonment, in addition to the fine.

In order to make a federal case for sale of narcotics, the government must prove three elements of the offense: (1) that the defendant sold the narcotics drugs, (2) that the narcotics drugs had been
imported contrary to law, and (3) that the defendant knew the narcotics drugs had been imported unlawfully.

Although the evidence may be adequate to sustain a state conviction, in order to justify a federal conviction the additional elements
of unlawful import and knowledge of unlawful import must be
proved.

Other federal narcotics offenses are the carrying of narcotics on
a vessel of the United States, while engaged on a foreign voyage, or
the using of a communications facility in an unlawful narcotics
transaction.

3. Narcotics Drug Record Keeping

Both federal and state law require that certain records be kept as
to the lawful possession, sale, and dispensing of narcotic drugs.
Failure to comply with these record keeping laws results in an
offense. Also, any fraud in the dispensing or using of narcotics drug
prescriptions is similarly punishable.

4. Hypodermic Equipment

Unless a person belongs to a specific exempted occupation, possession by him of a hypodermic syringe, hypodermic needle, or other
similar instrument designed to inject narcotic drugs is unlawful.
Usually exempt from this prohibition are, understandably: physi-
cians, dentists, chiropodists, veterinarians, nurses, embalmers, phar-
macists, research scientists, laboratory technicians or hospital em-
ployees acting under the direction of a physician or dentist, and a
manufacturer or dealer of hypodermic equipment for members of
the exempt group.

5. Glue Sniffing

In many states it is an offense to inhale the toxic vapors of any glue, cement or other adhesive containing specified chemical compounds, including acetone, benzene, alcohol, ether and others. It is also an offense to sell such compounds to any person whom the seller knows has the intention of unlawfully inhaling the toxic vapors.

Example
> The parents of Sam, a high school dropout, have warned Dan, the proprietor of a hobby shop, that Sam is an addicted glue sniffer and that Dan should not sell him any glue. In spite of this warning, Dan sells Sam twelve tubes of airplane glue. Later Sam is arrested while weaving up and down Main street sniffing the fumes of the airplane glue. Dan is also arrested. Both Dan and Sam are guilty of a criminal offense in those states which have anti-glue sniffing laws.

6. Narcotics Sold upon Prescription

If a narcotic drug is prescribed by a physician, dentist, chiropodist, or veterinarian, the dispenser (pharmacist) and user (patient), as well as the person who has prescribed the drug, are not in violation of the law.

Example
> Tom has an impacted wisdom tooth. His dentist prescribed codeine to relieve the pain. Tom takes the prescription to the local drugstore, where the pharmacist fills the prescription. All three individuals have acted within the law. If Tom were in a hospital, and the codeine was administered by a nurse, upon a physician's instruction, she too would have acted lawfully.

7. Narcotic Addiction: Crime or Illness?

The Supreme Court has held that since narcotic addiction is an illness, an addict cannot be criminally prosecuted for being an addict. To do so, said the Court, is a violation of the constitutional prohibition against "cruel and unusual punishment".

This ruling does not mean, however, that an addict is immune from the law prohibiting *possession* of narcotics. Nor does it mean that an addict is immune from punishment for offenses that he may commit in order to support his addiction financially.

Example

Bill and Bob are arrested while "high" from heroin. Both admit they are addicts. A tin foil packet containing narcotics is found on Bob's person. No drugs are found on Bill. Bill is guilty of no offense. Bob has violated the law solely because he was found to be in possession of narcotics and not because he was addicted or under the influence.

Example

Jack, a narcotic addict, is caught committing a burglary. At his trial he contends that his addiction compelled him to steal in order to secure the money needed to buy narcotics. His defense is invalid.

SECTION E. POSSESSION AND SALE OF DEADLY WEAPONS

The possession, use, and sale of dangerous weapons have long been the concern of law enforcement. Most laws relating to deadly weapons are based upon the rationale that, absent appropriate justification created by special circumstances, the possession, use, and sale of weapons inherently dangerous to human life constitute sufficient hazards to society to call for their prohibition. In addition, most state legislatures have decided that even weapons that are not inherently dangerous to human life also present a hazard to society when misused and that they too warrant appropriate restrictive legislation.

1. Weapons Absolutely Prohibited

The purchase, manufacture or possession of certain weapons are absolutely prohibited in many states. This category of weapons usually includes the following: machine gun, bludgeon, black-jack, slingshot, sand-club, sandbag, sawed-off shotgun, metal knuckles, switchblade knife, bomb, grenade, and "Molotov Cocktail".

2. Weapons Carried With Unlawful Intent

The possession of another category of weapons constitutes a criminal violation only if the possession is with an intent to use the weapon unlawfully, and the unlawful intent is usually inferred from the circumstances under which they are possessed. This category includes knives and razors.

3. Other Prohibited Weapons

The possession or use of tear gas projectors, stink bombs, spring guns, and silencers for firearms is either absolutely prohibited or else strictly regulated in most jurisdictions.

4. Carrying a Concealed Firearm

It is an offense for an individual to carry a revolver, pistol or other hand gun concealed on or about his person. In some jurisdictions it is an offense to carry any firearm, regardless of size, concealed on the person. Some states also make it an offense to carry a concealed hand gun or a firearm in an automobile.

The courts have held that where any part of the weapon is visible to the eye it is not "concealed" within the meaning of the law. In some states there is no offense for carrying a concealed firearm if the firearm is "not immediately accessible" to the person. A firearm is "not immediately accessible" where it is not within easy reach and under the control of its possessor.

Example

Bob, a cowboy from the West, visited a big Eastern city for the first time. Having heard the President speak about "crime in the streets" in the big cities, Bob carried his six-shooters in a double-holstered belt on the outside of his coat. while strolling in this manner down the main street, Bob was arrested and charged with carrying a concealed weapon. This charge was invalid. The firearms were not concealed; they were in open view.

If Bob's conduct was frightening or disturbing to the people who observed him, he might be charged with disorderly conduct, but not for violating a weapon law.

Example

Harvey was an avid member of a national pistol association. Exercising what he considered to be his "right to bear arms", as expounded in the association's bulletin, Harvey carried loaded pistols in the trunk of his car, in the locked glove-compartment, and under the driver's seat. Has he violated the law against carrying concealed firearms in an automobile? The firearms in the trunk and the locked glove-compartment are not concealed firearms within the meaning of the law since they are not "immediately accessible" to

Harvey. However, the pistol under the driver's seat is a concealed firearm within the meaning of the law since Harvey
can easily reach under the seat to gain control of the pistol,
making it "immediately accessible."

5. Unlawful Sale and Purchase of Firearms

Some states have laws which prohibit the sale of firearms to, or
the purchase of firearms by, certain categories of persons. These
include minors, ex-felons, individuals on probation, persons who are
mentally retarded, and narcotics addicts.

6. Groups Exempted from Deadly Weapons Prohibitions

Certain occupational groups are usually exempted from most of
the prohibitions dealing with deadly weapons. The most frequently
exempted groups are police, jail or prison guards, military, private
watchmen, target shooters, hunters, and members of veterans organizations.

7. Firearms Registration

Most jurisdictions have laws requiring a retail seller of firearms
to keep a register of all firearms sold or given away. The register will
usually contain the date of the sale or gift, the name, address, age,
and occupation of the person to whom the weapon is sold or given,
the price of the weapon, the kind, description and number of the
weapon, and the stated purpose for which it is purchased and obtained. This type of registration law permits law enforcement authorities to inspect the register and all stock on hand.

Some jurisdictions have recently enacted legislation requiring owners to register hand guns—or, in some instances, *all* firearms. These
laws provide for a criminal penalty for the possession or ownership
of an unregistered firearm.

At least one state has recently enacted a law requiring the licensing of all firearm *owners*. Ammunition may be purchased only upon
exhibiting a firearm owner's identification card. The law provides
for a criminal penalty for ownership or possession of a firearm by a
non-licensed owner.

In view of recent decisions of the Supreme Court of the United
States, there is a possibility that some state firearms registration or
licensing laws, if not carefully drafted, may be held unconstitutional
on the ground that they compel a person to do something that will

incriminate, or tend to incriminate him. For instance, he may have stolen the gun or used it in a killing or in some other crime.

Recent attempts to enact meaningful federal firearms registration or licensing have thus far met with failure.

8. Defacing Identification Marks on Firearms

Most states make it an offense to change, alter, remove or obliterate the name of the maker, model, manufacturer's number or other marks of identification on a firearm. Often the mere possession of any such firearm is considered as presumptive evidence that the possessor has changed, altered, removed or obliterated the identifying marks.

9. Offenses Committed While Armed with a Deadly Weapon

Most states invoke a stricter penalty for certain offenses where a deadly weapon is used in the commission of that offense. The most frequent offenses calling for aggravated penalties if committed while armed are robbery, assault, battery, and kidnapping. At least one state takes an even stricter approach and creates a separate and distinct offense, with a mandatory two year minimum penitentiary sentence penalty, for the use of a "dangerous weapon" in the commission of the offenses of kidnapping, rape, deviate sexual assault, assault, battery, intimidation, grand larceny, burglary, resisting a police officer, and escape from prison.

Section F.   Annoying and Dangerous Misconduct

There are some offensive activities which are too varied or too general to be outlawed in specific terms. For this reason a few statutes or code provisions have been rather broadly worded in order to cover such activities. Examples are the enactments entitled "disorderly conduct", or "disturbing the peace".

1. Disorderly Conduct and Disturbing the Peace

Legislative provisions under the labels of "disorderly conduct" and "disturbing the peace" seek to prevent persons from knowingly committing acts in such an unreasonable manner as to alarm or disturb another person or persons. The gist of the offense is not so much that a person committed an offensive act, but that he knew or should have known that it would tend to disturb, alarm, or provoke others. The emphasis is upon the unreasonableness of the conduct and its tendency to disturb. What is "unreasonable" depends upon the facts in each particular case.

Some of the general classes of conduct traditionally considered to be disturbing of the peace or disorderly conduct are: the creation or maintenance of loud and raucous noises of all sorts; threats to damage property or cause bodily harm; careless or reckless display of fireworks or of other dangerous instruments; and fighting of all sorts.

Example

John was upset because his former sweetheart Mary was marrying Bill. During the ceremony at the church wedding of Mary and Bill, John shot a pistol loaded with blanks into the air. This, of course, achieved his purpose of interrupting the ceremony. John was guilty of disorderly conduct. However, the same act of shooting a blank cartridge in the air would not be criminal under different circumstances (for example, if done in a desert).

Example

Harry went to the funeral of his old friend Fred after he had spent a few hours in a tavern. During the funeral service, Harry shouted, waved and sipped on a can of beer. This behavior would be disorderly conduct. However, under different circumstances (at the ball park, for example) this same conduct could be within the law.

Example

Phil ran through the aisles of the local theatre yelling "fire". The people in the audience became alarmed and vacated the theatre. Phil knew there was no fire. Phil was guilty of disorderly conduct. His conduct is unreasonable under these circumstances. If, however, there was in fact a fire, this same conduct would be proper.

In addition to the general language contained in most disorderly conduct statutes, some types of conduct are usually specifically prohibited. These prohibitions include: (1) the making of a telephone call, with intent to annoy another, whether or not a conversation thereby ensues; (2) the transmittal of a fire alarm knowing it to be false; (3) the transmittal of a warning that a bomb or explosive is concealed on a premises knowing the statement to be false; (4) reporting to a police officer that a crime has been or is being committed, knowing this statement to be false; (5) looking into a dwelling through a window for a lewd purpose.

2. Public Intoxication

A drunk weaving up and down on a sidewalk is another example of annoying misconduct, usually punishable under laws declaring it to be an offense to be in a public place while intoxicated. Enforcement is generally reserved to the individual who is not only drunk but whose conduct is of an annoying nature.

Although the Supreme Court has prohibited prosecutions for narcotic addiction, on the theory that such addiction is an illness, the Court has refused to prohibit prosecutions of chronic alcoholics for public intoxication. The difference between the two was the Court's conclusion that scientific evidence has not yet established that chronic alcoholism is an illness.

3. Mob Action, Unlawful Assembly, and Rioting

If a group of persons act in concert to perform certain acts, an offense may occur even though the conduct might not be criminal if performed individually. This type of offense is usually labeled mob action, unlawful assembly, or rioting. The size of the group required to make the conduct unlawful is a minimum of anywhere from two to twenty persons, depending upon the particular state statute involved.

Some unlawful mob action statutes contain a provision which permits the individual harmed to recover damages against the city, county or state in which the unlawful mob action occurred, as well as against members of the mob personally.

The activities proscribed by the unlawful mob action, unlawful assembly, and rioting statutes include: (1) the use of force or violence by a group of persons acting together and without authority of law which disturbs the public peace; (2) the assembly of a group of persons to do an unlawful act; (3) the assembly of a group of persons, without authority of law, for the purpose of doing violence to the person or property of anyone supposed to have been guilty of a violation of the law; and (4) the assembly of a group of persons, without authority of law, for the purpose of exercising by violence correctional powers or regulative powers over any person.

> *Example*
> The boys at Joe's tavern decided one evening to do something about the college students in town who were wearing

their hair long. The boys at Joe's all wore crew-cuts and felt
the long hair was feminine and Communist-inspired. All
twenty of them marched onto the campus and proceeded to
clip the hair, moustaches, and beards of all the men they
encountered. The boys' conduct may be punishable as mob
action. The individual crime of battery is also involved, of
course.

Example

The Joneses, a Negro family, moved into an all white
neighborhood. A gang of toughs stationed themselves outside
of the Joneses's home, vowing to "rough up" Mr. Jones if he
came out of the house. They are guilty of mob action.

Example

To call attention to slum conditions in a particular area, a
group of individuals band together and march down the
streets with flaming torches and threaten to burn down the
town if the slum conditions are not remedied. They are
guilty of rioting.

a. Looting

Out of public concern similar to that occasioned by riots, a few
states have recently enacted anti-looting laws. Looting occurs when
a person enters any building of another, in which normal security
of property is not present because of a hurricane, fire, act of God, or
riot, and attempts or accomplishes a theft of property.

Example

A city was paralyzed by a severe blizzard. As a result
neighborhood stores were not able to open and the police
were unable to patrol the streets. Joe and Bill observe a
storm-broken window at the Big X Liquor Mart. They helped
themselves to several bottles of liquor in the broken display
window. In addition to committing the offense of theft, Joe
and Bill would be guilty of the crime of looting.

4. Preventive Controls Over Citizens' Group Conduct: Parades and Marching Permits

A statute which calls for the procurement of a parade permit as
a condition for conducting a parade or march, and which leaves it to
the discretion of the officials to issue or refuse to issue the permit, is
constitutionally void as an infringement of First Amendment free-

doms of speech and assembly. However, parade permits with limited restrictions may be constitutionally acceptable.

Some of the permissible statutory restrictions for the issuance of a parade (or "march") permit might be:

(1) Limitations as to number of paraders (although such limitations, must relate to problems of pedestrian and vehicular traffic);

(2) Reasonable notice to law enforcement officers as to the names of the organizers, the time and place of the parade;

(3) Restriction of parade to non-peak traffic periods; and

(4) Restriction of nighttime parades into residential areas.

5. Restrictions on Residential Picketing

A few states have statutes which make it criminal to picket the residence of another person. However, usually no offense occurs: (1) where the residence is used as a place of business; or (2) where the residence is the place of employment and a person involved in a labor dispute is peacefully picketing; or (3) where the residence is the place of holding a meeting; or (4) where the residence is commonly used to discuss subjects of general public interest.

SECTION G. BRIBERY

The offense of bribery occurs when an individual, with intent to influence the performance of any act related to the employment or function of any public officer, public employee, or juror, promises or tenders to that person any property or personal advantage which he is not authorized by law to accept.

Example
John "slips" the clerk of a traffic court a five dollar bill in consideration of the destruction by the clerk of John's citation for drunken driving. John has committed bribery. (So has the clerk, as subsequently explained.)

In many jurisdictions, the fact that the person to whom the property or personal advantage is tendered does not in fact hold the position the offeror of the bribe assumes him to hold does not negate the offense.

Example
Mike attends a coroner's inquest into the death of a pedestrian struck by Mike's car. Mike sees a man in a white

coat outside the inquest room in the County Building, and
thinking that the man is a deputy coroner, Mike hands him
$500 and asks that the man make certain that the verdict of
the coroner's jury be "accidental death". The man in the white
coat was in fact an employee of the County Building cafeteria, who accepted the money without saying a word and
happily returned to the cafeteria kitchen. Mike has nevertheless committed bribery. In many jurisdictions, the employee
would also be guilty of bribery.

The offense of bribery occurs even though the offer of the bribe is
made to an intermediary and not directly to a public official or employee or juror.

Example

Paul, a liquor distributor, is charged with the offense of
gambling. George is a juror at Paul's trial. One morning during the course of the trial, Barbara, Paul's wife, met Gail,
George's wife, outside the courtroom and offered her several
cases of champagne if she would convince her husband to
vote for Paul's acquittal. Barbara has committed bribery. If
the juror's wife had accepted the offer of the champagne, she
would be guilty of bribery, regardless of whether or not she
communicated that offer to her husband.

The public official or employee or juror who either accepts a bribe
or solicits a bribe is also guilty of the offense of bribery.

Example

Alderman Phil tells the ABC Rug Company that, if ABC
provides free carpeting for his home, he will vote for an ordinance pending before the City Council which would rezone
a residential area so as to permit the ABC company to build
a modern rug warehouse. Phil is guilty of bribery.

A person who is not a public official or employee or juror, but does
not disabuse the offeror of this false notion that he holds such posi-
tions, would also have committed the offense of bribery in some
jurisdictions.

Example

Larry, after leaving a building which he has just burglar-
ized, runs into Jim whom he mistakes for a police officer.
Larry says, "Officer, if you let me go, I'll give you this $50
bill". Jim accepts the $50. In some states, he has committed
bribery.

The intermediary who accepts or solicits a bribe for a public official, employee, or juror, whether or not with that person's permission or knowledge, is guilty of the offense of bribery.

SECTION H. CRIMINAL USURY

Under civil law, a person or business which charges more than the legal rate of interest for a loan (usually 7% or more per annum) is in violation of the law. The civil consequences to the lender of a usurious loan, depending upon the particular state statute, are (a) the reduction of the amount of interest to the legal rate, (b) the loss of right to recover the interest, (c) the loss of both loan (principal) and interest, or (d) payment to the borrower of a penalty of an amount double or triple the usurious rate of interest.

In recent years, elements of organized crime have gone into the so-called "juice" loan business. This has made usury a serious criminal problem. A "juice" loan is one in which the borrower agrees to satisfy the loan with monthly or weekly payments at an interest ("juice") rate of a hundred or more per cent per annum of the principal. Thus, a borrower during the course of a relatively short period of time may make interest payments which total to 10, 20 or even a hundred times the amount borrowed. Borrowers who have failed to keep up with the interest or "juice" payments have been threatened, beaten, and even murdered.

In an effort to suppress the "juice" loan racket, several states have enacted criminal usury laws. These laws provide for a criminal penalty for the lender of loans at a rate considerably higher than the usury rate for civil purposes (the criminal usury rate is usually set at an amount greater than 20% per annum).

Example

Mickey has incurred some gambling debts. He meets Tony at his local bar and borrows $500 from him at the rate of 10% interest per week. Mickey pays Tony $50 interest per week for several weeks without reducing the $500.00 principal. He finds he is unable to keep up the payments. Mickey is not obligated to pay Tony the interest ("juice") payments. In some jurisdictions Tony would be further penalized civilly, for example, by loss of the principal. In many states Tony would also be guilty of the offense of criminal usury.

The criminal usury law does not apply to licensed small loan companies which are regulated by other state laws.

Example

Ed found himself indebted to several stores and companies. In order to pay off these debts and to have one monthly payment rather than more than 20, Ed borrowed $1000 from the Friendly Loan Company at an interest rate of 12% per month on the unpaid balance. Ed soon gets tired of making his monthly payments and goes to the Local Legal Aid Society for free legal advice in hopes of extricating himself from his obligations to the Friendly Loan Company. In most states Ed would be unhappy with the legal advice received. Although the interest rate he will be paying may be in excess of both the civil and criminal usury rates, his state probably has special small loan company licensing legislation which authorizes the business activities of the Friendly Loan Company. Ed may be comforted, however, by the knowledge that he will not be bruised or killed because of a failure to meet his obligations on the loan.

Chapter 4

Interference with Law Enforcement, and with Judicial and Other Governmental Processes

SECTION A. INTERFERENCE WITH POLICE OFFICERS

Many states have statutes which make it a crime to interfere with the duties of a police officer.

Example

Officer Jones observes Jerry, a bearded, 16-year-old hippie "peace-nik", throw a rock at marchers in an Armed Forces Day parade. When Officer Jones identifies himself and announces that Jerry is under arrest, Jerry runs away down a side street. Officer Jones gives chase, but is stopped by the actions of three of Jerry's friends who deliberately block Officer Jones's path, causing him to lose Jerry in the crowd. Jerry's three friends are criminally liable for their conduct.

Similarly, it is a crime, in many states, for a person, upon command of a police officer, to fail reasonably to aid in the apprehension of an individual or in the prevention of the commission of a crime.

Example

Officer Smith observes Edgar, a militant white Anglo-Saxon Protestant leader, looting a Bar-B-Que stand. Smith gives chase and Edgar runs to a taxi-stand and begins to enter the taxi of Driver A. Smith shouts his identity to A and orders A not to drive off. A, because he too is a WASP, disregards Smith's order and drives off. Smith then jumps into the taxi of Driver B and orders him to follow A. B, also a WASP, declines to do this. Both A and B are criminally liable for failing to aid Smith in the apprehension of Edgar.

65

SECTION B. OBSTRUCTING SERVICE OF PROCESS

The obstruction of the authorized service or execution of any civil or criminal court process or other order of the court is a violation of the law.

Example

Deputy Sheriff X goes to the high-rise apartment building of Reginald in order to serve a divorce summons upon him. Lloyd, the doorman, not wishing to permit any annoyance to Reginald, refuses to permit Deputy Sheriff X into the building on the pretext that X is not wearing a white shirt (X's uniform shirt is blue). Lloyd's conduct is criminal.

SECTION C. TAMPERING WITH EVIDENCE

It is a crime for a person, with intent to prevent the apprehension or obstruct the prosecution or defense of any person, to destroy, alter, conceal or disguise physical evidence or to plant false evidence or furnish false information.

Example

A and B, strangers to each other, meet at C's tavern and have a fist fight. B falls down and accidentally hits his head on a bar stool and dies. A flees the tavern. C, the bartender-owner, in order to protect his good customer A, gives a false physical description of the person with whom B was fighting. By so doing C has committed a crime.

SECTION D. PERJURY

Perjury occurs when a person makes a false statement under oath that is material to the issue in which the making of an oath is authorized by law.

Example

Walter testifies under oath at a liquor license revocation proceeding on behalf of the licensee tavern owner charged with a prostitution solicitation occurrence in his tavern. Walter states that he was in the tavern at the time and that no such solicitation occurred. However, it is later proved that not only did the solicitation occur as charged, but that Walter never was in the tavern. Walter committed perjury.

Example
> At a recess during a criminal trial for murder by shooting, Roy walked up to the judge and told him that the defendant was his brother-in-law and had admitted to him that he murdered the deceased. The prosecution informed the judge that Roy not only was unrelated to the defendant, but had never talked to the defendant who was in continuous custody from the moment of the shooting. Roy should not be tried for perjury; his statements were not made while under oath.

Perjury also occurs when a false statement is signed where the law requires it to be signed under affirmation and the falsity is material to a major element of the statement.

Example.
> State X requires that an application for a driver's license be signed under affirmation (and witnessed by a notary public). The application requires a statement as to the age of the applicant. A person must be under 70 years of age in order to obtain a license. Abner, 75 years of age, signs an application under affirmation and alleges he is 69 years of age. Abner has committed perjury.

A law may be enacted, however, prescribing that a false statement on a public document (e.g., driver's license, tavern license application, etc.) is punishable criminally, even though it is not sworn to. An income tax return is an example on the federal level.

Where someone makes contradictory statements under oath, the prosecution need not specify which statement is false. However, in many jurisdictions, if these contradictory statements are made in the same continuous trial and the witness admits the falsity of one of the statements, he will not be guilty of perjury.

Example
> In a personal injury trial, Gordon testified for the plaintiff on direct examination that the defendant drove his auto through a red light before striking the plaintiff. On cross-examination, Gordon stated the light was green. Gordon would be guilty of perjury, unless he admitted on cross-examination that his first statement was false.

Section E. Subornation of Perjury

A person commits subornation of perjury when he induces another to commit perjury.

Example
> If, in the previous example, the plaintiff's attorney induced Gordon to testify falsely that the light was red (after he had first told the attorney the light was green), the attorney would be guilty of the offense of subornation of perjury.

Section F. Prohibited Communications and Contacts with Jurors and Witnesses

It is a crime in most jurisdictions for a person to communicate in a manner other than that authorized by law with a person he believes to be a juror, with the intent to influence the supposed juror in regard to any matter which may be brought before him.

Example
> Nat is a neighbor of Carl, a juror in a case in which Dan, a friend of Nat's is on trial for a criminal offense. While the trial is still on, Nat remarks to Carl one Sunday that it is a shame that Dan is in trouble and that he has learned that Dan was "framed". Nat's conduct would be criminal in many jurisdictions.

In some jurisdictions, it is a crime to communicate with a juror or witness (or with a potential witness or juror) in such manner as to intentionally produce mental anguish or emotional distress.

Example
> John is sitting on a jury in a case involving an alleged assault on a non-union employee by a union employee, Jack. As John leaves his home each morning to go to court, several of Jack's fellow workers shout obscenities at John. This conduct would be criminal in some states. If the obscenities were vile enough, other criminal laws might also be violated.

Example
> Throughout the night before Will is to testify in a trial against a brother of Frank, Frank telephones Will periodically. Each time that Will answers the phone Frank hangs up with-

out saying anything. By trial time the next morning, Will is a nervous wreck from lack of sleep. In some jurisdictions, Frank's action would violate a specific state statute prohibiting this type of conduct.

It is a crime in most jurisdictions for a person to communicate threats, offers of reward, or false information to any witness or potential witness, with intent to deter the witness or potential witness from testifying freely, fully, and truthfully in any pending matter.

Example

Andy, a member of a juvenile gang, is on trial for assaulting a police officer. Bob, a neighborhood merchant, witnessed the crime from his place of business and is scheduled to testify. Clyde and Doug, fellow gang members, go to Bob's store and inform him that if Bob testifies at Andy's trial his store windows will be broken. Regardless of whether Clyde and Doug say that they, or some other party will break the windows, they are in violation of the criminal laws of many states.

Example

Under the factual circumstances of the example above, Clyde and Doug advise Bob, the neighborhood merchant, that they have learned that he will soon receive a package containing $1000 on condition that he not testify against Andy. Even though it is clear that the money is not coming from Clyde and Doug, the communication of the offer of reward is a criminal act in and of itself in many states.

Example

Again, under the same factual circumstances, Clyde and Doug tell Bob that he must have been mistaken in his identification of Andy since Andy was out of the city with them at the time of the crime. Although Clyde and Doug might testify to that effect at Andy's trial, the communication of this information to a potential witness with the intent of inhibiting his testimony would be against the law in many states.

It is a crime for a person, with intent to prevent the apprehension of, or to obstruct the prosecution or defense of, any person, to induce a witness having material knowledge to conceal himself or to leave the jurisdiction.

Example

 Tom and Candy are high school sweethearts. One evening in the heat of passion, while parked in front of Candy's home, Tom forcibly rapes her. Although her parents report the crime to the police, the parents begin to have second thoughts about prosecuting Tom. Prior to Tom's trial, Candy's parents take her to another state, temporarily, so that she will not have to testify against Tom, thereby assuring his acquittal. The conduct of Candy's parents is criminal.

In the preceding example, if Tom's parents had offered to pay for a trip to Europe for Candy in exchange for her failure to report Tom's crime to the police, both Candy's and Tom's parents would have been guilty of "compounding a crime". (Other examples of compounding a crime were presented in an earlier section of this book, under the subject of *Theft*.)

It is also a crime in many states for a person who, with intent to prevent the apprehension or obstruct the prosecution or defense of any person, conceals himself or leaves the state in order to avoid testifying.

Example

 In the same preceding example, if Candy voluntarily left the state because she did not wish to testify against Tom, she would be guilty of a crime.

Chapter 5

Uncompleted Criminal Conduct and Criminal Combinations

There are three crimes, called "inchoate" offenses, for conduct that falls short of a completed act—attempt, solicitation, and conspiracy.

Section A. Attempt

A person commits the crime of attempt when he: (1) intends to commit a specific offense, and (2) performs an act which is a substantial step toward its commission. "Mere preparation to commit a crime" does not constitute a "substantial step toward its commission". The courts hold that the difference between conduct which is a "substantial step" and that which is "mere preparation" is one of degree, and must be determined by the circumstances of each case.

Example
> John, a domestic, purchased some cyanide and put some of it in a hot chocolate he intended to serve to his employer Harold. John anticipated that he would be named as a beneficiary in Harold's will. John's actions were discovered prior to Harold's drinking of the hot chocolate. John is guilty of the offense of attempt to murder.

Example
> Bob flunked his medical boards and, disgruntled, decided to go into the illegal abortion business. He purchased surgical equipment for this activity, but abandoned the idea before making contact with any prospective patients. Bob has not taken a "substantial step" toward completing the offense of abortion. His "mere preparation" is not criminal.

In most jurisdictions, it is not a defense to the crime of attempt that because of a misapprehension of the circumstances it would have been impossible for the accused to commit the crime attempted.

Example

Tim fired a pistol at Hal with intent to kill him. However, someone without Tim's knowledge had loaded the pistol with blanks. The fact that this made it impossible to kill Hal did not negate Tim's offense of attempt to murder.

SECTION B. SOLICITATION

A person who, with intent that an offense be committed, commands, encourages or requests another person to commit that offense is guilty of the crime of solicitation.

Example

Mack gets into an argument with the bartender at his local tavern and is ejected when he becomes too boisterous. Furious at what has occurred, he offers a passing teenager $10 to throw a brick into the tavern window. Mack is guilty of the offense of solicitation to commit criminal damage to property.

SECTION C. CONSPIRACY

The offense of conspiracy occurs when two or more persons agree to commit a crime. Some states require also that in order for the crime to occur, at least one of the conspirators must commit an overt act in furtherance of this agreement.

Example

Tom, Dick and Harry, local hoodlums, meet at Tom's home and agree that Dick will beat up Joe who has been late with his "juice loan" payments to the trio. Tom phones Joe and tells him that his son has been struck by an automobile and is at the hospital. Dick then trails Joe as he leaves his home for the hospital intending to assault him along the way. But before any harm can be done to Joe, Dick is picked up by the police. Tom, Dick, and Harry have committed conspiracy. In some jurisdictions, it would not have been necessary for Tom to phone Joe—or for Dick to trail him—in order to satisfy all the elements for the offense of conspiracy.

It is no defense to the crime of conspiracy that one or more of the conspirators were not prosecuted, or were acquitted, or were convicted of a different offense, or fled the jurisdiction, or lacked the capacity to commit the offense. Therefore, in the foregoing example, if Dick was not prosecuted or if he was acquitted, Tom and Harry still could be tried for conspiracy. Similarly, if Dick was convicted of attempted battery, the others could be tried for conspiracy nevertheless. And if Dick was mentally incompetent or had fled to Brazil, Tom and Harry could still be tried for conspiracy.

Chapter 6

Accessories to a Crime

Although there is no legal concept in this country of "guilt by association" as such, under certain circumstances an individual may be criminally liable for the acts of another person.

SECTION A. ACCESSORY BEFORE THE FACT

Broadly stated, a person who aids or assists another in the performance of a criminal act is regarded as an "accomplice" or as an "accessory before the fact". In most states he is subject to the same penalty as the individual who performed the criminal act.

One state deals with this kind of conduct by means of the following statutory provision:

"When one person engages in conduct which constitutes an offense, another person is criminally liable for such conduct when, acting with the mental culpability required for the commission thereof, he solicits, requests, commands, importunes, or intentionally aids such person to engage in such conduct."

Following are excerpts from another state statute, which contains a provision for use in cases where an accessory has a timely change of mind and acts to prevent the criminal conduct:

"A person is legally accountable for the conduct of another when:

". . . either before or during the commission of an offense, and with the intent to promote or facilitate such commission, he solicits, aids, abets, agrees or attempts to aid, such other person in the planning or commission of the offense. However, a person is not so accountable, . . . if:

> ". . . before the commission of the offense, he terminates his effort to promote or facilitate such commission, and does one of the following: wholly deprives his prior efforts of effectiveness in such commission, or gives timely warning to the proper law enforcement authorities, or otherwise makes proper effort to prevent the commission of the offense."

Example

X, Y and Z agree to rob the City Bank. X drives Y and Z to the bank. Y and Z, armed with pistols and wearing masks, enter the bank and hold it up. X, unarmed, waits in the car for Y and Z. Y and Z are arrested with the loot as they leave the bank. Later X is picked up. X argues that he did not enter the bank and rob it, was unarmed, and never was in possession of any of the loot. X's argument is futile. He is equally liable with Y and Z under the law for the offense of robbery.

Example

A and B, syndicate hoodlums, receive a "contract" to murder C. B changes his mind hours before the murder is to take place and telephones a warning to C. He also alerts the police. In spite of these warnings, A successfully shoots and kills C. B, by his efforts to prevent the commission of C's murder, terminated his liability for A's criminal action.

Section B. Accessory After the Fact

A person who, with intent to prevent the apprehension of an offender, conceals his knowledge that an offense has been committed or harbors, aids or conceals the offender is regarded under the law as an "accessory after the fact" and is punishable under the law. The penalty for the "accessory after the fact" is usually less than that for the principal offender.

Following is an illustration of legislation bearing on this kind of conduct:

> "Every person not standing in the relation of husband, wife, parent, child, brother or sister to the offender, who, with intent to prevent the apprehension of the offender, . . . harbors, aids or conceals the offender, shall be fined not to exceed $1,000

or imprisoned in a penal institution other than the penitentiary
not to exceed one year or in the penitentiary from one to 2
years, or both fined and imprisoned".

Example

   X is wanted by the police as a suspect in the commission
of a crime. He goes to the home of his friend Y and tells
him he is wanted and must hide. Soon thereafter, the police
knock on Y's door. Y hides X in a closet and tells the police
X is not there. Later Y drives X to the bus station and purchases a ticket for him for a destination out of town. Y is
criminally liable as an "accessory after the fact".

Chapter 7

Principles of Criminal Responsibility

There is a general principle of criminal law to the effect that a person cannot be held criminally responsible for an act unless that act was accompanied by an "evil-meaning" mind. In other words, a prohibited act is ordinarily not punishable unless performed with what is variously described as "criminal intent", "felonious intent", "malice aforethought", "fraudulent intent", "wilfulness", or "guilty knowledge", etc. This restrictive principle, however, is confined to serious offenses. Certain other acts—the relatively minor ones—may be punishable even in the absence of an "evil-meaning" mind.

Example
X, a customer leaving a restaurant, takes a coat off a coat rack, puts it on and walks off with it. It belonged to someone else, but X mistook it for his own, and did not realize his mistake until the owner caught up with him several blocks away. X is not guilty of larceny or any other criminal offense.

Example
Y is stopped by a traffic officer for crossing an intersection without stopping. Y said he did not see the stop sign. His failure to see it is no defense.

In general, it may be said that where the prohibited act is a relatively minor one, and where the social need to discourage the particular kind of conduct would be severely jeopardized by the difficulty of proving the evil-meaning state of mind, then the courts will permit guilt to be proved merely upon the basis of the act alone.

Section A. The Defense of Infancy

In earlier days the very young were not exempt from punishment as criminals. A ten-year-old boy, for instance, was convicted and executed for killing his companion, as was a child of eight who had burned down a barn. Under modern concepts, however, a person under a certain age (thirteen in some states) is considered incapable of harboring an "evil-meaning" mind and, therefore, immune from criminal prosecution. Children under that age, of course, are subject to juvenile court proceedings, and may be placed in non-penal institutions for their own welfare and for the protection of others.

Section B. The Defenses of Compulsion and Necessity

A person who is compelled by someone else to do a criminal act may invoke the defense of compulsion, but not if it involves the taking, or an attempt to take, the life of an innocent person.

Necessity may compel a person to take another's personal property, or to intrude upon his real property, and he too may have a valid defense. For instance, a hunter caught in a severe snowstorm and without needed food, will not be guilty of burglary or larceny if he breaks into a cabin and consumes what is required to keep him alive.

Section C. The Defense of Intoxication

A person who is so intoxicated that he does not know what he is doing is not criminally liable for an offense for which *specific intent* is an element. In other words, if he picks up another's property and makes off with it he may successfully defend himself on a charge of larceny if the court or jury decides that his intoxication was of such a degree that he could not have entertained the intent to deprive the owner of his property permanently. On the other hand, the intoxication defense is not available if the offense is one involving only general intent, or recklessness. For example, a motorist who kills someone while driving recklessly because of his intoxication, cannot defend by saying that he did not know what he was doing.

Section D. The Insanity Defense

According to a long established rule, a person is not criminally responsible for an act committed while he was in an "insane" state of mind.

One of the earliest, and certainly the best known of the early tests of insanity, was that laid down in the famous *M'Naghten* case in 1843. In that case the English House of Lords ruled, basically, that although every person is presumed to be sane, no one could be held criminally responsible for an act if at the time of its commission— *and due to a diseased mind*—he did not know "right from wrong".

For many years the M'Naghten "right-wrong" test was the one that prevailed throughout the United States. Then it was supplemented by the "irresistible impulse" test. In other words, even though a person knew "right from wrong" he could not be held criminally responsible, if, because of a disease of the mind, he was unable to avoid doing wrong.

In recent years two other tests have been tried. One that emanated from the Federal Circuit Court for the District of Columbia—the *Durham* test—was widely applauded at the time, but only one other jurisdiction has adopted it; and it has been rejected by other Federal Circuit Courts. Moreover, it has since been modified very considerably in its practical case-by-case application. Essentially the *Durham* rule stated that a person could not be criminally responsible if the act he committed was "the product" of a mental disease or defect.

The most popular test today, and the one that is gaining more and more acceptance is the so-called A.L.I. test—a test formulated and proposed by the American Law Institute. That test reads as follows:

1. A person is not responsible for criminal conduct if at the time of such conduct as a result of mental disease or defect he lacks substantial capacity either to appreciate the criminality of his conduct or conform his conduct to the requirements of law.
2. The terms "mental disease or defect" do not include an abnormality manifested only by repeated criminal or otherwise anti-social conduct.

A person who is found to have been insane by any of the foregoing tests will be acquitted of the offense charged against him. However, if mental examinations conducted after his acquittal establish that he should be placed in a mental institution for care and treatment he may be thus committed in a civil proceeding.

Section E. Mental Incompetency to Stand Trial and at Time of Execution of Sentence of Death

Irrespective of the state of mind of an accused person at the time of the act he is alleged to have committed, he cannot be brought to trial if, at that time, his mental condition is such that he is "unable to understand the nature and purpose of the proceedings against him, or to assist in his defense". In such situations he would be committed to a mental institution and could only be tried thereafter if and when his mental condition improves sufficiently to satisfy the above two requirements.

In death penalty cases there can be no execution if prior to the time of the scheduled event the sentenced person had developed a mental condition that will not permit him "to understand the nature and purpose" of the sentence of death.

Part III

THE LEGAL RULES GOVERNING POLICE PRACTICES AND PROCEDURES

Chapter 8

Arrest

Any contemplated discussion of the legal rules governing police practices and procedures immediately poses the problem of where to start and what should come first. For instance, although "stop-and-frisk" frequently is the first step in a police procedure that may ultimately result in a criminal prosecution, it is difficult to understand the legal limitations upon that particular police practice without knowing the legal limitations upon an actual arrest. Moreover, by reason of recent United States Supreme Court restrictions upon police interrogations the question arises as to what may be asked of a person who has been stopped for investigation, or arrested—and under what conditions and circumstances. Also involved in both "stop-and-frisk" and arrest situations, is the issue of when, and under what circumstances, may the police search for or seize incriminating evidence, either from the person, from his car, or from the area where the stopping or the arrest occurs.

The best starting point, we believe, is with a discussion of *arrest*— its definition, the conditions under which the police may make an arrest, and the consequences of an illegal arrest.

"Arrest" has been variously defined. The following are illustrative:

> "Arrest is the taking of a person into custody in order that he may be forthcoming to answer for the commission of an offense." *American Law Institute Code of Criminal Procedure*, § 18.

> ✻ ✻ ✻

> "'Arrest' means the taking of a person into custody," and it may be made "by an actual restraint upon the person or by

his submission to custody." *Illinois Code of Criminal Procedure,* §§ 102–5, 107–5.

* * *

"An arrest is the taking of another into custody for the actual or purported purpose of bringing the other before a court, body or official, or of otherwise securing the administration of the law. . . . Mere words will not constitute an arrest, while on the other hand no actual physical touching is essential . . . an assertion of authority and purpose to arrest followed by submission of [the person] constitutes an arrest. There can be no arrest without either touching or submission." *Perkins, Elements of Police Science* 227 (1942).

"Arrest" does not include the questioning of a witness to a crime who is not in custody. Nor does it cover a situation where a motorist is stopped for a check of his driver's license or of car ownership; nor even when he is stopped for the issuance of a traffic ticket for speeding, etc. Only when "custody" occurs does the stopping escalate into an arrest; in other words, only when the police officer conveys an intention to take the person to the police station or before a judicial magistrate.

There are two forms of arrest—arrest without a warrant, and arrest with a warrant.

Section A. Arrest Without a Warrant

A police officer may make an arrest without a warrant when he has "probable cause" to believe a suspect has committed a crime. Some state statutes phrase this "probable cause" test in terms of "reasonable grounds", or "reasonable cause", to believe that the arrestee has committed an offense, but they are considered the equivalent of "probable cause".

The "probable cause" requirement stems from the provision in the Fourth Amendment to the United States Constitution, and from comparable state constitutional provisions, protecting persons from "unreasonable seizures" and requiring that "no warrants shall issue, but upon probable cause". The two provisions have been read to mean that an arrest without a warrant, as well as one with benefit of a warrant, must be upon "probable cause", for otherwise it would be "unreasonable".

Probable cause does not mean actual knowledge. Thus, the officer need not have personally observed the commission of the crime. He need only have knowledge of facts and circumstances which would lead a reasonable man to conclude that the suspect in all probability has committed a crime.

1. The Required Evidence for Probable Cause

The amount of proof necessary to satisfy the "probable cause" test is less than that which is required to prove in court that the suspect committed the crime. At the accused's trial, the prosecution must present evidence to prove him guilty beyond a reasonable doubt. To make an arrest, however, a police officer need only show "probable cause"; that is, enough facts to cause him to believe, upon reasonable grounds, that the suspect has committed an offense.

Following are two examples of "probable cause":

Example
Officer P, while cruising in his patrol car, heard a female voice from an alley yelling "Help! Thief!" Seconds later he observed S running down the alley away from the place from which he had heard the shouts for help. P chased S and apprehended him. P had "probable cause" to arrest S, even though subsequent events established his innocence.

Example
A police officer, cruising at 3 A.M. in a neighborhood which had recently experienced a number of burglaries, observes S walking down an alley carrying a portable TV set, a small leather case and several other objects. When S sees the police car he drops the items he was carrying and starts to run away. The officer has "probable cause" to arrest him.

Mere suspicion or a hunch will not, however, justify an arrest.

Example
S, who has a reputation for being a dope peddler, was seen by Officer P walking hastily to get into a cab. The officer arrests and searches him for narcotics. Officer P's action was not based upon probable cause and the arrest and search are illegal.

2. Hearsay Evidence and Informer's Tips

Under most circumstances, "hearsay" evidence, which may be loosely described as second-hand evidence, cannot be used at the trial of an accused person. However, if corroborated in some way, it may be used to establish probable cause for an arrest.

Hearsay evidence is most often in the form of information received by a police officer from an "informer". But the hearsay must be corroborated in either of two ways:

If a police officer observes certain activities, facts or circumstances, which substantiate the tip given by an informer, probable cause may exist for an arrest.

> *Example*
> X tells Officer P that S is selling policy tickets on a street corner. The officer, in an unmarked parked car, observes S conducting some sort of transactions with about twenty persons who have come up to him separately in the course of thirty minutes. As the individuals came up to S they each gave him something and he handed them something. Although Officer P could not tell exactly what was exchanged, his observations, coupled with the informer's tip, gave him probable cause to arrest S.

If a police officer has a contact with an informer who had previously given him consistently reliable tips in the past, he may rely upon such a tip to make an arrest.

> *Example*
> X tells Officer P that he observed S selling narcotics to Y. X describes S and tells where he will be that night for the purpose of making his sales. Upon several prior occasions whenever X gave Officer P such information P always found narcotics on the person "fingered" by X. Under these circumstances Officer P has probable cause to arrest S.

Of interest in connection with the hearsay evidence situations is the fact that, where an informer has furnished such information, his identity need not be disclosed at the suspect's trial, *unless*

(a) the informer himself participated in the crime; or
(b) the informer was a witness to the particular crime for which the arrest was made; or
(c) the informer was present at the time of arrest.

3. Consequences of an Invalid Arrest Without Warrant

There are several consequences of an invalid arrest by a police officer:

1. An invalid arrest will result in the suppression and exclusion, at the trial, of any evidence obtained as a result of that arrest. (The rationale behind this "exclusionary rule" is the discouragement of illegal police actions.)

2. An invalid arrest may also result in:
    (a) a successful false arrest action against the arresting officer;
    (b) a successful federal civil rights action against the arresting officer in the federal courts; and
    (c) departmental disciplinary action.

However, an invalid arrest, by itself, will not result in the acquittal of an accused person whose guilt can be proved beyond a reasonable doubt by other independent evidence; that is, evidence "untainted" by the invalid arrest.

Section B. Arrest With Warrant

The legal requirements for an arrest made pursuant to a court warrant are the same as those for an arrest without a warrant. Both must be based upon probable cause.

A warrant may be obtained by presenting to a judge or magistrate a "complaint" (a charge) made under oath, which contains statements that establish probable cause that the person named in the warrant committed the crime therein described.

(For illustrations of the forms used for arrest complaints and for arrest warrants, see appendices B, C, and D.)

The same kind of evidence that may establish probable cause for an arrest without a warrant (*e.g.*, hearsay bolstered by other factors, as previously described) may also justify the issuance of a warrant by a judge or magistrate.

The following example shows probable cause for the issuance of an arrest warrant:

> *Example*
> C is a hotel keeper. X tells him that S performs acts of prostitution in her hotel room. X says that he too had engaged S's services. Upon several occasions, C observes six men enter and leave S's room at intervals of about half an hour. Such information, submitted by C under oath, would justify an arrest warrant.

Following is an illustration of an absence of probable cause for the issuance of a warrant:

> *Example*
> X, a brother-in-law of Officer P, tells P that he heard from several persons that Miss Y was engaging in prostitution in

her room in the Hotel Rex. Without more information, Officer
P's affidavit of what his brother-in-law told him would not
justify an arrest warrant.

The following complaint is based *wholely* on hearsay and does not
show "probable cause":

Example

> Complainant C stated that Informant I told him that Sus-
> pect S was a receiver of stolen property. C then stated in
> detail, without corroboration, the alleged illegal transactions
> of S as told to him by I.

In cases where corroboration of an informant's tip is unavailable,
the only recourse is to have the informant himself sign the complaint. This is seldom done, however, because the complaint and the
warrant are public records, without the protection of anonymity;
and most informants are unwilling to run the obvious risks of dis-
closure of their identities.

Some jurisdictions will permit an informant-complainant to use an
alias in signing the complaint for an arrest warrant. But if he becomes a witness at the trial itself, he would be required to disclose
his own name.

1. Police Obligations in Warrant Arrests

What are the legal obligations and responsibilities of a police officer who is assigned to make an arrest pursuant to a warrant?

Where the warrant has been issued upon the sworn complaint of
another officer or upon the sworn complaint of the victim of a crime,
or of a witness, the officer who is to make the arrest is not required
to check into the warrant's total validity. He need only look to see
that it is signed by a judge or magistrate, that it contains the name
of the person to be arrested, and that it names the charge for which
the arrest is to be made. If the warrant is "fair on its face", as the
expression is sometimes used, the officer can proceed to effect an
arrest. He is privileged to assume the warrant was based upon probable cause since that determination was the responsibility of the
judge or magistrate who issued it.

On the other hand, the police officer who prepares the complaint
and drafts the warrant should realize that the probable cause requirement must be satisfied, and he should also make certain that all
of the state statutory requirements have been met. In some states

(for example, Indiana, as of 1969), the statutory requirements are very strict—perhaps overly strict and impractical. Compliance is nevertheless required.

Although the execution of a faulty warrant will not subject the arresting officer to civil or criminal liability, the arrest itself will be invalid and any evidence seized incident to the arrest will be suppressed and unusable at the trial.

Not every irregularity in a warrant will invalidate it—only those that adversely affect the substantial rights of the suspect. Following are examples of both inconsequential and consequential irregularities:

Example
The name of the person to be arrested was spelled correctly as "John Q. Smith" in six out of the seven places where it appeared in the complaint and warrant. In one place it was incorrectly spelled as "John Q. Smythe". The warrant is valid.

Example
The state arrest warrant statute required all complaints be "sworn to". Complainant C told Police Officer P about the crime committed by S. P prepared a complaint for C's signature. However, in the excitement of preparing the case, P neglected to make sure the complaint was sworn to prior to P executing the warrant of arrest. The judge who signed the warrant also neglected to notice that the complaint was not under oath. After S was in custody, P presented the complaint to the judge and it was sworn to by C at that time. This irregularity affects S's substantial right to be arrested on the basis of a warrant issued on a *sworn* complaint. The arrest is invalid.

The arrest warrant must be signed by a judge or magistrate. Most state statutes also require that the magistrate first "examine" the complainant as to the matters set forth in the complaint. For this reason, it is good practice to *always* bring the complainant to the judge's courtroom when presenting the complaint to the judge or magistrate for the issuance of a warrant.

As a security precaution against some clerk, bailiff, or other person "tipping off" the person to be arrested, the judge or magistrate may be requested to conduct the arrest warrant hearing in the privacy of his chambers. Sometimes he may even conduct it in his home or at some other place away from the courtroom.

Even though time and circumstances may have afforded the police an opportunity to obtain an arrest warrant, an arrest may nevertheless be made without one whenever there exists the probable cause to do so. In other words, although there are situations where a warrant arrest may be considered advisable, there is no compelling legal necessity for a warrant where the requirement of probable cause can be otherwise established.

> *Example*
>   Police Officer A and Police Officer B went to the home of S for the purpose of arresting him. They had known of his illegal activities for several days. Officer A thought that Officer B had signed a complaint and secured a warrant arrest prior to arriving at S's home. B thought A had done this. Neither A nor B had in fact procured the warrant. The arrest of S is nevertheless proper because both A and B had "probable cause" to arrest S without a warrant.

Although it is advisable, where circumstances permit, for the arresting officer to have the warrant of arrest with him at the time of arrest, the modern general rule is that it is not essential that this be done. In fact, any officer who has reasonable grounds for believing that a warrant has been issued may make a valid arrest of the person who has been named in a warrant.

2. Consequences of an Invalid Arrest Warrant

Where counsel for the arrested person seeks to attack the validity of a warrant he will file in court, before trial, what is known as "a motion to quash" the warrant of arrest. If he is successful—that is, if the motion is granted—the arrest will be declared illegal and any evidence obtained incident to the arrest will be suppressed and unusable at the trial. In most such incidences, there will be no trial, because of the fact that no case can be proved against the accused without the evidence that was suppressed.

> *Example*
>   S was arrested for robbery-murder pursuant to a warrant based upon an unsworn complaint. When the officers searched S they found a loaded pistol in his pocket. Subject to the exception in the next example, the pistol could not be used as evidence either at the robbery-murder trial or at a trial upon a charge of carrying a concealed weapon.

Where a warrant is declared void because of a substantial defect, the arrest itself might still be valid, and the seized evidence admissible at the trial, if the circumstances under which the arrest was made would have justified an arrest *without* a warrant.

Example

A warrant was obtained for the arrest of S on a charge of rape of a child. Officer P, looking for S near S's home, observes him pick up another child in his car and speed off. Officer P gives chase and ultimately arrests S. In his car, and in clear view of Officer P, there is a child's garment that was later identified as belonging to the raped child. On S's trousers there is a stain that is later determined to be blood of the same type as that of the rape victim. Even though the arrest warrant may contain a defect and be declared invalid, the garment and the blood evidence would be admissible at the rape trial, because under the foregoing circumstances Officer P could have made a valid arrest without an arrest warrant.

As previously stated, the arresting officer is protected against any civil or criminal liability when he acts with the benefit of a warrant, even though it should ultimately be declared invalid.

Section C. The Area (Jurisdiction) in Which a Police Officer May Exercise His Arrest Powers

1. Jurisdiction in Non-Warrant Case Situations

In the absence of a special law to the contrary, a police officer may only arrest for "probable cause" in the jurisdiction of his particular police department. Therefore, a state police officer may arrest on probable cause throughout the state. A county police officer, however, may only make an arrest in the county of his department, and a city officer only in the city which his department serves.

Nevertheless, a police officer who observes a suspect commit a crime in his jurisdiction may chase that suspect into another jurisdiction and make the arrest there. This is commonly called the doctrine of "fresh pursuit" or "hot pursuit".

Example

X and Y are adjoining municipalities. P is a police officer in X, and while on patrol he observes S snatch a purse from a woman on a street in City X. S jumps into a car and drives away. P chases him on his motorcycle. S makes it to City Y, where Officer P curbs S's car and arrests him. The arrest is valid even though P is a police officer in City X and not in City Y.

A police officer who is outside of his own jurisdiction may effect a lawful arrest in his capacity as an ordinary citizen. (The conditions under which citizen arrests may be made will be discussed in a following section.)

2. Jurisdiction in Warrant Case Situations

In many jurisdictions a warrant of arrest may be executed by any police officer of the state in which it was issued. However, a police officer in one state may not execute an arrest warrant in another state. To apprehend an out-of-state suspect or fugitive, legal proceedings must be commenced for his extradition from the other state. A federal arrest warrant, however, may be executed by a federal officer in any state.

Section D.   Force Permissible in Effecting an Arrest

A police officer may use that force which he reasonably believes to be necessary to make the arrest and to protect himself or another person from bodily harm while making the arrest. However, in most jurisdictions a police officer may not use force which is likely to cause death or great bodily harm in making an arrest *for a misdemeanor* unless that degree of force is necessary to protect the police officer or another person from death or great bodily harm at the hands of the person to be arrested.

Following is an illustration of the use of *excessive* police force in making an arrest.

Example

Officer P observes juvenile J steal several quarters from a newsstand and begin to ride away on his motor bike. P is on foot. P fires his revolver at the fleeing J. Officer P used excessive force in seeking to apprehend J.

A private citizen in making an authorized arrest may use the same force as a police officer. However, he usually may not use force which is likely to cause death or great bodily harm, *even in the case of a felony,* unless that degree of force is necessary to prevent him or another person from death or great bodily harm at the hands of the person to be arrested.

SECTION E. POST-ARREST POLICE OBLIGATIONS

The laws of practically all jurisdictions require that when an arrest is made without a warrant, the arrestee must be taken before the nearest judge or magistrate "without unnecessary delay". When the arrest is pursuant to a warrant the arrestee must be taken before the judge who issued the warrant, or, in his absence, before the nearest judge or magistrate in the same county.

"Unnecessary delay", as used in the various statutory provisions, is generally interpreted to mean a delay for any reason other than the unavailability of a judge or magistrate, or circumstances such as distance, lack of ready transportation, etc. Some state courts give the phrase a more liberal interpretation, by saying that it means only an *unreasonable* delay, and consequently the police are permitted to retain custody over an arrestee for a *reasonable* length of time, with reasonableness being determined by all the surrounding circumstances of the particular case.

Example

S is arrested by the police of City Y at 10 o'clock in the morning as he leaves the scene of a burglary. The police put him in a jail cell and keep him there until 10 o'clock the next morning, even though a judge was in a courthouse six blocks away. Such a delay is "unnecessary", and "unreasonable".

Example

Five persons observe two men commit a robbery in a tavern at 2 P.M. One of the witnesses, W, was shot in the foot as a result of an accidental discharge of the gun of one of the robbers. The police apprehend suspect A, who fits the description of one of the robbers, but they cannot locate A's brother B who fits the description of the other one, and who has a criminal record for robbery. The police retain custody of A as they continue the search for B and as they wait for W's release from a hospital so he and the other witnesses can view A in a "line-up". The next morning, after B is apprehended, and all five witnesses have viewed both suspects in "line-ups", A and B are taken before a judge. The delay is "necessary" and "reasonable".

The reason for this rule which prohibits "unnecessary" or "unreasonable" delays in taking an arrestee to a judge or magistrate is to afford him a judicial determination as to whether there are reasonable grounds for continuing to hold him in custody. The procedure for determining this is known on the state level as a "preliminary hearing"; in the federal system it is referred to as an "arraignment".

SECTION F. ARRESTS BY FEDERAL OFFICERS

There is no single act regarding the arrest powers of federal officers generally. The matter is dealt with by separate statutes pertaining to particular groups of officers. For instance, there is a separate provision for F.B.I. agents which authorizes an arrest, without warrant, for "any offense against the United States committed in their presence, or for any felony cognizable under the laws of the United States if they have reasonable grounds to believe that the person to be arrested has committed or is committing such felony". Another statute confers a similar power upon marshals and their deputies. Still another prescribes such arrest rights for agents of the Bureau of Narcotics. The various arrest rights of members of the Secret Service are also separately defined, as is the case, too, regarding members of other governmental units such as the Bureau of Prisons, etc.

SECTION G. CITIZEN ARRESTS

For certain crimes, and under certain conditions, a private citizen may make an arrest. The scope of his arrest power and the limitations upon it are usually specified in state statutes or in municipal or county ordinances. As a general rule, he may arrest for "a crime" committed "in his presence". Generally excluded as offenses for which citizen arrests can be made are violations of municipal or county ordinances. Also exempt in some states are misdemeanors.

Perhaps the range of citizen arrest powers can best be indicated by quoting from the statutes of the following states: California, Illinois, Louisiana, and New York:

California

A private person may arrest another:
   1. For a public offense committed or attempted in his presence.

2. When the person arrested has committed a felony, although not in his presence.
3. When a felony has been in fact committed, and he has reasonable cause for believing the person arrested to have committed it. (§ 837, Penal Code.)

Illinois

Any person may arrest another when he has reasonable grounds to believe that an offense other than an ordinance violation is being committed. (§ 107–3, Illinois Code of Criminal Procedure, 1963.)

Louisiana

A private person may make an arrest—
(a) For a felony committed in his presence;
(b) When the person to be arrested has committed a felony although not in his presence;
(c) When summoned by any peace officer to assist said officer in making an arrest. (West's La. Rev. Stats. § 15:61.)

Arrest for offense other than felony: To justify an arrest for any misdemeanor, breach of the peace, or violation of any ordinance committed or attempted in the presence of him making the arrest, said arrest must be made at the time of such commission, or of such attempt, for, except for felony, no one can legally make an arrest, without a warrant, for anything previously done or attempted in his presence. (§ 15:62.)

(Changed in new code, essentially to (b) only.)

New York

A private person may arrest another,
1. For as offense, committed or attempted in his presence;
2. When the person arrested has committed a felony, although not in his presence. (§ 183, N.Y. Code of Cr. Proc.)

Citizen Assistance in Police Arrest

In some states a citizen is bound by law to assist a police officer in making an arrest, if the officer commands him to do so. An illustration of this is to be found in the Illinois Code of Criminal Procedures, which provides that "a peace officer making a lawful arrest may command the aid of male persons over the age of 18" and the person so commanded "shall have the same authority as that of a peace officer". The code also provides that the assisting person "shall not be civilly liable for any reasonable conduct in aid of the officer".

Section H. Legal Alternatives to Arrest

Most jurisdictions have alternatives to arrest for taking a suspect into custody to stand trial for a crime. These alternatives are (a) a *notice to appear* and (b) a *summons*. They are most commonly used in traffic offenses. For example, the hang-on parking ticket instructing the owner of an automobile to appear in court on a specific date to answer charges is a *notice to appear*. Also, the ticket given by an officer to a motorist for a moving violation is a *summons* ordering the motorist to appear in court on a specific date to answer charges. The consequences of ignoring either *summons* or *notice to appear* is usually the issuance of a warrant for the arrest of the offender.

The *notice to appear* and *summons* have in recent years been used by some jurisdictions with increased frequency in non-traffic crimes. These procedures are especially effective for use in (a) cases of minor crimes and (b) cases where the suspect is a responsible member of the community and there is little or no expectation that he will flee the jurisdiction prior to his trial date.

Chapter 9

Search and Seizure

Under specific circumstances a police officer may search a suspect and seize articles on the person of or in the area in the immediate presence of the suspect. If the search is proper, the items seized may be used in evidence against the suspect at his criminal trial. However, if the search is improper, the items seized will be "suppressed" and cannot be used at the trial. For this reason, it is important for a police officer to know the scope of his authority to make a search and seizure. In addition, the making of an improper search and seizure could subject a police officer to civil liability, as well as to an undesirable performance rating within his department.

SECTION A. SEARCH INCIDENT TO ARREST WITHOUT WARRANT

In connection with a *lawful* arrest on view, that is, without an arrest warrant, a police officer may search a suspect and the area in the suspect's immediate presence. The arrest, of course, must be lawful in order for the search to be valid. Also, there must be a valid purpose for making the search. Some of the purposes which will justify a search are the following:

(A) A police officer may search the arrested person for the purpose of protecting the officer from attack.

> *Example*
> Officer Jones makes a lawful arrest of Clyde in Clyde's automobile. Jones had reasonable grounds for believing Clyde had committed a burglary.
> A search may be made of Clyde for a weapon. Moreover,

97

Jones can search for burglary loot inside the car and the trunk.

(B) A police officer may search the arrested person for the purpose of preventing him from escaping custody.

Example

Officer Smith arrests Joe at the scene of a burglary. Before placing Joe into the police car, the officer may search him for any weapon or instrument which might be used by Joe in attempting to escape from custody.

(C) A police officer may search the arrested person for the purpose of discovering the fruits or evidence of the offense, or for any instruments, articles or items used in the commission of the offense.

Example

Officer Brown gives undercover agent X some marked money to purchase narcotics. X enters a tavern, while Brown remains outside. X gives Sam the marked money and receives a sealed packet in return. X turns the packet over to Brown outside the tavern. Brown field-tests the contents of the packet and decides that it is heroin. Brown enters the tavern and arrests Sam. Brown may search Sam to recover the marked money and other packets of heroin which may be on Sam's person. The marked money is the fruit of the crime and it, as well as the packets of heroin, constitute evidence of the offense of sale of narcotics.

Example

Bill is arrested in his rented room for the forcible rape and robbery of a high school girl earlier that day. The arresting officer, in most jurisdictions, would be justified in searching through Bill's nearby soiled laundry for blood or semen-stained underwear worn by Bill at the time of the offense. Such items would be evidence at the trial for forcible rape. In any jurisdiction, the officer would have authority to search Bill and the area within easy reach for the items taken from the girl during the robbery (fruits of the offense).

Even though an arrest is valid, there can be no search if one of the above-described purposes for the search does not exist.

Example

Officer White properly arrests A for "jay walking." White does not know A and A's actions have not been otherwise

suspicious. White searches A and finds an obscene photograph in A's pocket. This search was improper and if A
were tried for possession of obscene material, the photograph
would be suppressed.

The fact that the police officer has grounds to obtain an arrest or
a search warrant, and that there is ample time to secure the warrant,
does not make improper a search which can be justified as incident
to a lawful arrest on view without a warrant.

Example
In the rape case above, Bill at his trial argues that the
evidence seized at his apartment should be suppressed, since
the arresting officer had an opportunity to secure an arrest
or search warrant and had ample time to do so. If probable
cause existed for Bill's arrest, the fact that time permitted the
procurement of warrants is of no consequence.

In making a search incident to the execution of a defective arrest
warrant or based upon a defective search warrant, the search may
be valid, even though the warrant itself is defective, as incident to
an arrest without warrant.

Example
In the same case, if the arresting officer had searched Bill
incident to the execution of a faulty arrest or a search warrant, the search still could be justified as incident to a valid
arrest on view, since the officer had probable cause for
making such an arrest.

Section B. Search Incident to Arrest Upon Warrant

A police officer may search a suspect for any of the previously described purposes (A, B, and C of the preceding section) when executing a legally proper arrest warrant. The officer, in most jurisdictions,
need not have the arrest warrant in his possession at the time of the
arrest and search, provided that a legally proper arrest warrant has
been issued and the arresting officer has knowledge of that fact.

Example
Officer A has been instructed at the department's morning
roll call that an arrest warrant has been issued for Z. A,

while walking his beat, sees Z. A may arrest Z on the basis
of the warrant and may search Z if there are factors present
which justify the search: (a) to protect A, (b) to prevent
Z's escape and (c) to discover any evidence or fruits of the
crime or items used in its commission.

Section C. Duration of the Search

A lawful search may continue until, but only until, the purpose of
the search has been satisfied.

Example

Undercover agent A, using marked money, purchased
narcotics from Suspect B in the living room of B's apartment.
Thereafter B was arrested by the police in the living room of
his apartment. A search of the living room led to the discovery
of marked money and more narcotics. After this discovery,
the police continued the search for three more hours, during
which search they discovered some stolen property under the
floor boards of the bedroom closet floor. The seizure of the
money and narcotics was proper because they were under B's
immediate control and the purpose of the search was to discover these fruits of the crime. However, after recovery of
these "fruits", the extended search was improper and for that
reason the stolen property was improperly seized.

Section D. Time of the Search

The search must be made contemporaneously with the arrest to
which it is incident. A search of the surroundings within the suspect's immediate control should also be made in the presence of the
suspect.

Example

Officer A arrested B in B's apartment. A took B in custody
to the police station. Later that evening A returned to B's
apartment and made the search. The search was improper.
It either should have been made at the time of B's arrest and
in B's presence or Officer A should have secured a search
warrant for the subsequent search.

Under some state statutes, an automobile used in the commission
of an offense, such as a narcotics violation, may be seized by the po-

lice authorities. Under authority of this type of legislation, a police officer may seize an auto and its contraband contents subsequent to the time of arrest.

SECTION E. PLACE AND PREMISES TO BE SEARCHED

The police may search the premises under the control of the arrested individual as well as his person. Therefore, if a man is arrested in his car or apartment, an appropriate search may be made of the area of the car or of the apartment in his immediate control. However, if a man is arrested on the street, he may not be taken to his car or apartment in order to search those places.

Example
Suspect F was arrested on the street outside his apartment building. The police officers forced him to take them to F's apartment where they "formally announced" that he was under arrest and searched the apartment "incident" to that arrest. The search was improper. The arrest occurred outside of F's apartment and the police could not search the apartment without a search warrant.

SECTION F. FORCE USABLE IN A SEIZURE

A police officer may use reasonable force and employ reasonable means to seize evidence during a search.

Example
The police officers arrested Suspect J for a narcotics violation. On seeing the officers, J attempted to swallow two narcotics capsules he was carrying. The officers grabbed J and shook him and forced him to cough up the capsules before he could swallow them. The police conduct was reasonable and proper.

Example
In the same situation as above, J actually swallowed the capsules. The police officers took J to the hospital and ordered that J's stomach be pumped (without J's consent) in order to retrieve the capsules before they dissolved. This police conduct was excessive and unreasonable, and therefore the seized evidence would be suppressed.

Section G.　Consent Searches

A search may be legalized by the consent of the person to be affected by it or by someone authorized to act in his stead.

One question that has yet to be resolved by the United States Supreme Court is whether a warning of constitutional rights as to searches and seizures, similar to the *Miranda* rule regarding confessions, must first be given in order to obtain a valid consent to search. The court decision law thus far has been to the effect that no such warning is required.

A relative who lives with a suspect may consent to the search of jointly inhabited premises on the rationale that both parties have an equal right to the use and possession of the premises.

> *Example*
>
> The defendant, in custody after his arrest for murder, told the police where the murder gun could be found. The defendant's wife met the police at the door of the defendant's home and consented to the search. The search and seizure of the murder gun was with consent and therefore valid.

The rule permitting a consent search by a joint tenant to bind a non-consenting joint tenant applies even though the co-tenants are not husband and wife or otherwise related. In the absence of a familial relationship the existence of an equal right to use and possession may be inferred when the consenting person has a property right or other connections with the premises, or with the defendant, in such a way as to signify that he is entitled to bring guests into the premises. In other words, it must be adequately shown that the consenting party had a right equal to that of the non-consenting defendant to use and possess the premises being searched.

> *Example*
>
> R's girl friend, who occasionally spent the night at R's apartment, consented to the search of R's apartment while R was away. This was not a valid consent and the search was improper. There was no evidence of conduct on the part of the defendant or the girl suggesting that they had equal rights in the apartment or joint control over it; there was no proof that she had a key to the apartment or that she either brought her friends into it or had the authority to invite them; nor was there proof that she shared his board as well as his bed or that she resided with him in the apartment.

Under most circumstances, a hotel keeper may *not* validly consent to a search of the room of a guest or tenant. Nor can a landlord give a valid consent with regard to rented premises.

SECTION H. "PLAIN VIEW" SEIZURES OF CONTRABAND

Objects or materials which are not subject to lawful possession—in other words, "contraband" such as narcotic drugs—may be seized if they are within "plain view" of a police officer in a place where he is lawfully present.

Example

Officer Burns observes Pete walking down the street. Pete threw away a package. Burns retrieved the package which appeared to contain narcotics. The contents were field-tested and were found to be heroin. Pete was then arrested. The package was admissible into evidence at Pete's trial for sale of heroin since it was not taken by search and seizure, but was within the "plain view" of Officer Burns.

Example

Officer O'Malley, equipped with a warrant to search Alfredo's summer home for gambling paraphernalia, observes in "plain view" a sawed-off shotgun. Since its mere possession is unlawful the gun may be seized.

SECTION I. SEARCH WARRANTS

As with an arrest upon an arrest warrant, a search may be authorized by a judge or magistrate upon the issuance of a search warrant.

A search warrant may be executed without at the same time effecting an arrest. In other words, the search warrant is not conditioned upon or otherwise linked with any arrest action. Indeed, there are times when the owner of the car or premises to be searched may be in custody already, or he may be many miles away. Upon occasions, however, arrests are made at the time of, or following, a search executed pursuant to a warrant.

1. Things Subject to Seizure

At one time, in most states, the things that could be ordered seized in a search warrant were very limited, and generally to the instrumentalities of the crime (*e.g.*, gun), or the fruits of the crime (*e.g.*, the

stolen property). Today, however, the search warrant statutory provisions of many states permit the seizure of additional items,
such as:

   (1) Any instruments, articles or things used in the commission
       of an offense. For example, a revolver used in a murder.
   (2) Any instruments, articles or things which may constitute
       evidence of an offense. For example, a blood or semen-
       stained undergarment worn by a rapist.
   (3) A kidnap victim, for example, a hostage taken by a robbery
       suspect.
   (4) A human fetus. For example, in an abortion investigation.
   (5) A human corpse. For example, in a murder investigation.

2. Form of the Complaint for Search Warrant

A complaint for a search warrant must be signed under oath or
affirmation by either a police officer or a private citizen. This person
is called the "affiant" or "complainant". The complaint must state
facts to show probable cause that the item to be seized will be found
on the person or place described in the complaint. The complaint
may be based in part on corroborated hearsay if there is "a substantial basis for crediting the hearsay".

   Example
       Jones told the complainant, police officer Brown, that a
   gambling operation was being run at a specified premises.
   Jones showed Brown a betting slip he allegedly received at
   the gambling operation. Jones had given Brown reliable information on previous occasions. Brown surveyed the suspect
   premises and observed known gamblers coming and going.
   Brown's complaint for search warrant, with the hearsay supplemented by the corroboration of the information given to
   him by Jones, was adequate for the issuance of a search
   warrant.

The facts to show probable cause may be obtained by an affiant
who is an undercover plainclothes police officer.

   Example
       Officer Green, in plain clothes, visited Joe's Cigar Store
   and asked where he could place a bet. He was invited to the
   rear of the cigar store where a wire room was operating.
   Green, although in disguise, was not a trespasser. Since he
   made no "affirmative misrepresentation" and had been invited
   to a place "open to the public", his complaint for a warrant
   was valid.

The complaint for search warrant must particularly describe the place or persons to be searched and the things to be seized. The complaint (and the warrant based upon it) must leave the police officer who will execute it with no doubt as to precisely where to search and specifically what to seize.

The premises where the search is to occur must be described with such detail as to exclude any other premises. The address, apartment number, apartment location, and any other descriptive data should be detailed. Usually a slight error in the address, however, will not invalidate the complaint.

Example

The complaint described the premises as Apartment 2B in a three story red brick building with the address of 2300 S. State Street. This description was correct, except for the fact the correct address was 2310 S. State Street. However, there was only one building (the subject premises) on the 2300 block of South State Street. The description was adequate.

The complaint must describe with particularity what is to be seized. General and broad descriptions are inadequate. This is especially important in obscenity cases.

Example

The complaint stated that at Edna's book store, the owner kept "dirty, prurient, obscene and offensive books" underneath the counter. This description is inadequate. The complaint should state the title of the books and contain other descriptive data such as author, type of book, etc. If at all possible a copy of the book should be attached to the complaint. (It should also be recalled from the earlier discussion on obscenity, that special, speedy court procedures to determine the obscenity of books seized are also required.)

Where the search warrant is for the search of a building or other place, the complaint need not identify the person in charge of it. Nor does it have to name the person in possession of the things to be seized, or the particular offender.

(For illustrations of the forms used for search warrant complaints and for the search warrants themselves, see appendices E and F.)

3. The Form of the Search Warrant

Most of the descriptive data of the complaint (place to be searched and objects to be seized) must be repeated in the warrant. However, a search warrant will not usually be quashed (nor evidence suppressed) because of technical irregularities not affecting the substantial rights of the accused.

Example

 The warrant listed the bookmaker and person in charge of the premises as "Charles F. Smith" in 3 out of the 4 places where his name was mentioned. In the fourth place in the warrant, his name was inadvertently stated as "Charlie Smith". The warrant will not be quashed.

However, major defects (as discussed in preceding sections) will render the warrant void and constitute grounds for suppression at trial of the seized items.

4. Issuance and Execution of the Search Warrant

A reasonable delay between the date the items to be seized are first observed and the date of the issuance (signing by the judge or magistrate) of the search warrant does not render the warrant void. However, the better procedure is to apply for a search warrant immediately upon learning of the evidence that should be seized.

The warrant must be executed (served and the search made) within a reasonable time after the time of issuance (usually within three or four days). It may be executed either at night or during the day.

The length of time during which the search is conducted will not affect the validity of the search warrant. Nor will the validity of a warrant be affected by the fact that an invalid search without warrant is made contemporaneously with the search based upon the warrant itself.

Example.

 Police officers obtained a valid search warrant to search Apartment 25 of the Jet Hotel. They proceeded to the Jet Hotel and searched Apartment 25. While they were at the hotel, they also searched Apartment 26, without lawful authority. The unlawful search of Apartment 26 does not affect the validity of the search of Apartment 25 pursuant to warrant.

All necessary and reasonable force may be used to effect an entry into any building or property to execute a search warrant. When executing a search warrant, a policeman may reasonably detain and search any person in the place at the time, in order to:

(1) protect himself from attack, or
(2) prevent the disposal or concealment of any instruments, articles or things particularly described in the search warrant.

The United States Supreme Court has recently held that building, health and similar municipal inspectors must secure search warrants in order to inspect a premises whenever the party in lawful control refuses the inspector entry.

SECTION J. THE SUPPRESSION OF ILLEGALLY SEIZED EVIDENCE

If evidence is seized upon the basis of an invalid search, the defendant may move to suppress it (keep the seized evidence out of his trial). In most jurisdictions, this motion must be made before trial, but if the defendant was not aware of the grounds for the motion before trial, the motion to suppress may be made during trial when the prosecution seeks to introduce the evidence. In a few states, if the judge allows the motion and suppresses the evidence, the state may appeal from this ruling. Such an appeal does not constitute a violation of the defendant's protection against "double jeopardy", because jeopardy does not attach until the defendant is put on trial.

The motion to suppress evidence may be made during a civil proceeding, as well as a criminal proceeding, *if* the civil proceeding is "quasi-criminal" in nature, i.e., "almost" a crime, because of a possible "penalty or punishment" of some sort to the defendant.

Example.

State A has a statute providing for the forfeiture of an automobile to the state when the automobile is used for the transportation of narcotics. Joe Pusher is improperly arrested in his automobile and the automobile is unlawfully searched. During this search narcotics are discovered in the glove compartment and seized. State A files a civil proceeding to forfeit Pusher's automobile and during this proceeding the seized narcotics is sought to be used as evidence. The trial judge would have to suppress the evidence of the improperly seized narcotics.

Chapter 10

Criminal Interrogations and Confessions*

The cruelty and injustice involved in the early practices of extorting confessions from accused persons by tearing their bodies apart on a rack, or by inflicting other forms of torture, led to the development of certain precautionary court rules regarding the admissibility of confessions. What came to be required was that the confession must have been voluntary—a confession obtained by methods that were not likely to make an innocent person confess. In other words, it had to be a trustworthy confession.

In recent years, the United States Supreme Court has attached other conditions to the admissibility of a confession. In 1943, the Court held that no confession could be used as evidence in a *federal* criminal case if it had been obtained by federal officers during a period of "unnecessary delay" in taking the arrested person before a federal commissioner or judge. If the officers delayed the arrestee's "arraignment" (the equivalent of a "preliminary hearing" in state courts) for the purpose of interrogating the arrestee, a confession obtained during the period of delay would be suppressed and rendered unusable at the trial—regardless of its otherwise voluntariness or trustworthiness.

In laying down this rule of exclusion, the Supreme Court did not say that it was constitutionally required; the Court merely said that it was doing so in the exercise of its "supervisory power" over lower federal courts.

* For a description of the tactics and techniques of criminal interrogation, and for a detailed discussion of the law governing interrogations and confession admissibility, consult Inbau & Reid, *Criminal Interrogation and Confessions* (2d ed. 1967), published by the Williams & Wilkins Company, Baltimore, Maryland 21202.

Recently, because of an intense dissatisfaction with the practical consequences of the foregoing rule, Congress abolished it, as it was privileged to do, since it was not based upon any constitutional provision. In the same Act, however, Congress said that although police delay in presenting an arrestee to a judicial officer would not nullify a confession the factor of delay could be taken into account in determining the confession's voluntariness.

The climax to the Supreme Court's restrictions upon confession admissibility was reached in its 1966 five to four decision in *Miranda v. Arizona*.

SECTION A. PRE-INTERROGATION WARNINGS OF CONSTITUTIONAL RIGHTS

In the *Miranda* case, the majority of the Court held that whenever a person who is about to be interrogated by a law enforcement officer *"has been taken into custody or otherwise deprived of his freedom in any significant way"*, he must be given the following warnings:

(1) That he has a right to remain silent, and that he need not answer any questions;
(2) That if he does answer questions his answers can be used as evidence against him;
(3) That he has a right to consult with a lawyer before or during the questioning of him by the police; and
(4) That if he cannot afford to hire a lawyer one will be provided for him without costs.

All of the warnings must be given in such a way that the suspect clearly understands what he is being told.

If the suspect indicates, at any time, or in any manner whatsoever, that he does not want to talk, the interrogation must cease. The interrogator is no longer privileged to "talk him out of" his refusal to talk.

If the suspect says, at any time, that he wants a lawyer, the interrogation must cease until he has the opportunity to confer with a lawyer, and no further questions may be asked of him outside the lawyer's presence or without the lawyer's permission. Nor can the interrogator "talk him out of" his desire for a lawyer.

In instances where the suspect requests a lawyer but he cannot obtain one, and no lawyer is provided for him by the police, the interrogation must be terminated.

1. The Meaning of "Custody"

The meaning of the expression "in custody or otherwise deprived of his freedom in any significant way", which the Supreme Court used in the *Miranda* case, was somewhat clarified in a March 25, 1969 decision in the case of *Orozco v. Texas*.

The defendant, Orozco, was involved in a quarrel outside a tavern. A shot was fired, killing the other participant. The defendant left the scene and went to his boarding house. At about 4 A.M. four police officers arrived at the boarding house and were admitted by an unidentified woman. They were told that the defendant was asleep in his room. The officers entered the room and began to question him. He was asked if he had been to the particular tavern and he answered "yes". He was also asked if he owned a pistol and he admitted owning one. After being asked twice where the pistol was he told the officers it was in the washing machine in a backroom of the boarding house. The pistol was found there and laboratory tests established that it was the one which fired the fatal bullet.

At no time did any of the officers give the defendant the *Miranda* warnings, although, as one officer testified, the defendant was not free to leave the presence of the officers, and he was considered "under arrest".

A majority of the Supreme Court held that the defendant was "in custody" at the time the incriminating statements were made and therefore he was entitled to the *Miranda* warnings. Consequently, the defendant's statements about the pistol and his presence at the tavern were inadmissible as evidence.

The dissenting opinion in the Orozco case said that the "straitjacket" which had been imposed on law enforcement by the *Miranda* rules was now drawn "even tighter". The dissenting justices were of the view that the questioning of Orozco was not in station house "isolation", or in "unfamiliar surroundings", or in a "police-dominated atmosphere", about which the Court expressed its concern in the *Miranda* decision.

According to the dissenting opinion's interpretation of the Orozco decision *"once arrest occurs, the application of Miranda is automatic"*.

2. Waiver of Self-Incrimination Privilege and Right to Counsel

Under the Miranda decision, the only time a police interrogation can be conducted of a suspect who is in custody or otherwise restrained of his freedom in any significant way is *after* he has been given the warnings, and *after* he has expressly stated that he is willing to answer questions without a lawyer being present.

Once a valid waiver has been obtained from a suspect, a police interrogator may proceed to interrogate him, if there is no violation of the rule prohibiting an "unnecessary delay" in taking the individual to a judge or other judicial magistrate. In interpreting the meaning of "unnecessary delay", the state courts have given the police much more leeway than have the federal courts.

Section B. General Guidelines for Police Interrogators

Even after the Miranda warnings are given, and even after a valid waiver has been obtained from the suspect, the police interrogator will be faced with still another issue: what interrogation tactics and techniques are permissible in an effort to ascertain whether the suspect is telling the truth, or in an effort to obtain a confession from him if he is guilty?

Until the courts or the legislatures become more specific as to what is or is not permissible, we suggest that the police interrogator rely upon the following guideline with regard to the tactics and techniques he may use—by asking himself:

> *"Is what I am about to do, or say, apt to make an innocent person confess?"*

If a fair answer to the question is "no", the interrogator should go ahead and do or say what was contemplated; on the other hand, if the answer is "yes", he should refrain from doing or saying what he had in mind.

Example

Officer Jack, after encountering difficulty in persuading Suspect X to tell the truth, believes that X will tell the truth by being told that if he keeps on lying he will be hit over the head with a telephone book until he does tell the truth. The idea should be abandoned, for various reasons, one of which is to avoid the risk of obtaining a confession from an innocent person.

Example

Officer Bill, in interrogating Suspect Y, is asked by Y, "What will happen to me if I tell you I did this?" Bill thinks it will help if he tells Y that usually a person gets a very light sentence if he tells the truth, and that he, Officer Bill, will ask the prosecuting attorney to go easy on Y because of his cooperation. Any such statement will nullify a resulting confession, as measured by our suggested guideline. A person caught in a web of incriminating circumstances might well confess rather than run the risk of incurring a severe sentence.

Example

Officer John is questioning Z who is suspected of killing his wife. John thinks it will be helpful to sympathize with Z for the miserable treatment he had received from his wife over the years. This John may do. No innocent person will confess a murder because of this expression of sympathy.

Following is a list of various tactics and techniques which we believe should be sanctioned under our suggested general guideline. The list is from the Table of Contents of the second (1967) edition of *Criminal Interrogation and Confessions* by Fred E. Inbau and John R. Reid. (Published by the Williams & Wilkins Co., Baltimore, Md. 21202.)

Tactics and Techniques for the Interrogation of Suspects whose Guilt is Definite or Reasonably Certain

A. Display an air of confidence in the subject's guilt.
B. Point out some, but by no means all, of the circumstantial evidence indicative of a subject's guilt.
C. Call attention to the subject's physiological and psychological symptoms of guilt.
D. Sympathize with the subject by telling him that anyone else under similar conditions or circumstances might have done the same thing.
E. Reduce the subject's guilt feeling by minimizing the moral seriousness of the offense.
F. Suggest a less revolting and more morally acceptable motivation or reason for the offense than that which is known or presumed.
G. Sympathize with the subject by (1) condemning his victim, (2) condemning his accomplice, or (3) condemning anyone else upon whom some degree of moral responsibility might conceivably be placed for the commission of the crime in question.
H. Utilize displays of understanding and sympathy in urging the subject to tell the truth.

I. Point out the possibility of exaggeration on the part of the accuser or victim or exaggerate the nature and seriousness of the offense itself.

J. Have the subject place himself at the scene of the crime or in some sort of contact with the victim or the occurrence.

K. Seek an admission of lying about some incidental aspect of the occurrence.

L. Appeal to the subject's pride by well-selected flattery or by a challenge to his honor.

M. Point out the futility of resistance to telling the truth.

N. Point out to the subject the grave consequences and futility of a continuation of his criminal behavior.

O. Rather than seek a general admission of guilt, first ask the subject a question as to some detail of the offense, or inquire as to the reason for its commission.

P. When co-offenders are being interrogated and the previously described techniques have been ineffective, "play one against the other".

Tactics and Techniques for the Interrogation of Suspects Whose Guilt is Uncertain

Q. Ask the subject if he knows why he is being questioned.

R. Ask the subject to relate all he knows about the occurrence, the victim, and possible suspects.

S. Obtain from the subject detailed information about his activities before, at the time of, and after the occurrence in question.

T. Where certain facts suggestive of the subject's guilt are known, ask him about them rather casually and as though the real facts were not already known.

U. At various intervals ask the subject certain pertinent questions in a manner which implies that the correct answers are already known.

V. Refer to some non-existing incriminating evidence to determine whether the subject will attempt to explain it away; if he does, that fact is suggestive of his guilt.

W. Ask the subject whether he ever "thought" about committing the offense in question or one similar to it.

X. In theft cases, if a suspect offers to make restitution, that fact is indicative of guilt.

Y. Ask the subject whether he is willing to take a lie-detector test. The innocent person will almost always steadfastly agree to take practically any test to prove his innocence, whereas the guilty person is more prone to refuse to take the test or to find excuses for not taking it, or for backing out of his commitment to take it.

Z. A subject who tells the interrogator, "all right, I'll tell you what you want, but I didn't do it," is, in all probability, guilty.

Although we cannot assure interrogators that all confessions obtained by the employment of the general guideline we have recommended will be admitted in evidence, it is the only understandable and reasonable one we can offer. It is also the only test, in our opinion, that is fair both to the suspect and to the law abiding public.

Section C. The Future for Criminal Interrogations

Congress, in 1968, incorporated a provision into the "Omnibus Crime Control and Safe Streets Act", which was aimed at relieving federal officers (and indirectly state officers) from most of the United States Supreme Court's restrictions upon police interrogations, and particularly the ones imposed in the Miranda case. Basically what the new Congressional act does is to reestablish "voluntariness" as the test of confession admissibility; however, in determining "voluntariness" consideration would still be given to such factors as lack of warning about the self-incrimination privilege and right to counsel, as well as the elapsed time from arrest to arraignment. No one factor's absence, however, would serve to nullify a confession.

Whether the Supreme Court will uphold the constitutionality of this Act of Congress is questionable.

Chapter 11

"Stop-and-Frisk"

Although the police practice of stopping and frisking persons whom they reasonably suspect of criminality is a long-standing one, the constitutional authorization for it, and the legal limitations upon the practice, were shrouded with uncertainty until the 1968 United States Supreme Court decision in *Terry v. Ohio*. Although this decision did not dispel all of the uncertainty, it did sanction the "stop-and-frisk" practice in general and in it the Court did attempt to lay down some understandable rules for the police to follow.

Section A. Legal Guidelines for "Stop-and-Frisk"

In the Terry case the Court held that where a police officer

(1) "observes unusual conduct which leads him reasonably to conclude in light of his experience that criminality may be afoot and that the persons with whom he is dealing may be armed and presently dangerous", and

(2) "in the course of investigating this behavior he identifies himself as a policeman and makes reasonable inquiries", and

(3) "nothing in the initial stages of the encounter serves to dispel his reasonable fear for his own or others' safety",

the officer "is entitled for the protection of himself and others in the area to conduct a carefully limited search of the outer clothing of such persons in an attempt to discover weapons which might be used to assault him".

As is readily apparent, the Court's language strictly limits the circumstances that justify the "stop" and the scope of the "frisk". Unless all of the prerequisites spelled out by the Court are met, an investigating officer's conduct will lack legal validity, and, among other possible consequences, a seized weapon would be suppressed as evidence.

Following are case situations illustrating proper as well as improper "stop-and-frisk" practices:

Example

Tom, Dick and Harry were observed by Officer Jones standing and conferring on a street corner. The three men took turns walking to a jewelry store half-way down the block. One suspect would look into the store and report back to the other two. The men kept their right hands in their respective overcoat pockets a good deal of the time. Jones approached the men, identified himself and inquired as to their names and the reason for their being in the area. They said nothing (or else they gave an implausible explanation). Jones "frisked" them and recovered revolvers from their overcoat pockets. Jones' "stop and frisk" of the three suspects was proper, and the evidence seized is usable.

Example

For several hours Officer Smith observed Sam standing in front of a restaurant. During this time Sam spoke with eight known addicts. He entered the restaurant and spoke with three more addicts. Smith entered the restaurant, identified himself, told Sam to come outside and said, "You know what I am after". Sam mumbled an inaudible response and Smith reached into Sam's pocket and pulled out several glassine envolopes of heroin.

Smith's action was improper because (1) he acted not for his own protection, but was merely searching for narcotics, and (2) he exceeded his authority by immediately reaching into Sam's pockets without first "patting him down".

Example

Millie was a beauty contestant from Turkey in the Miss World Contest held in Des Moines, Iowa. Officer Sherlock posed as a judge in the beauty contest in order to gather information as to narcotics which were being smuggled into Des Moines from the Middle East. Sherlock, in order to get a date with Millie, led her to believe he would vote for her. They parked in Sherlock's car. He noticed a strange bulge in Millie's toreador pants. Thinking it was a Mid-eastern sabre, he proceeded to "pat her down". Wishing not to offend the contest judge, Millie let Sherlock "pat her down" until she discovered that in the process he had recovered the sabre and heroin as well. Sherlock's conduct was improper. He was required to identify himself as a police officer.

Example

There were several strong-arm robberies by juveniles in the 19th Police District. On Saturday night Captain Tracy saturated the district with officers and set up a "dragnet". During the evening 100 youths were "stopped and frisked". This police action was improper because there were no reasonable grounds to believe that any particular youth was involved in criminal activity.

SECTION B. FIELD INTERROGATIONS AND WARNINGS OF CONSTITUTIONAL RIGHTS

When a police officer stops a person for investigation, must he give the Miranda warnings regarding the right to remain silent and the right to counsel?

In our opinion, we believe that in ordinary "stop-and-frisk" situations the warnings are not required. On the other hand, if in any particular case the circumstances justify an actual arrest, or if it can be said that the suspect reasonably believed he was being placed under arrest, then the warnings are probably necessary. The following case situations are illustrative:

Example

Officer Brown observed Nick carrying a suitcase and walking tippy-toe and barefooted down the hallway of Brown's apartment building at 4:00 A.M. Brown did not recognize Nick as a tenant of the building. Brown identified himself and asked, "what are you doing?" Nick remained silent for a while but finally replied: "You got me. I just broke into Apartment 4G". At his trial Nick's attorney argues that Nick's confession of burglary should not be used against him because he had not been warned of his constitutional rights before making the statement to Brown. This contention is unjustified because Nick was not under arrest. Brown's action constituted only a "stop". So the Miranda warnings need not have been given. However, if instead of observing Nick walking down the hall, Brown had seen him "jimmying" the door of 4G, the Miranda warnings would have been required, because Brown would have then made an arrest rather than merely a "stop".

SECTION C. THE EFFECT OF A SUSPECT'S FAILURE TO REPLY

A person who is "stopped and frisked" is not required to answer a police officer's questions. There exists the constitutional right to remain silent. However, if the circumstances are such that an innocent person would likely respond with a simple explanation of his actions, the suspect's failure or refusal to do so may be considered along with all other evidence in determining whether there are grounds for arrest.

Example

Officer Jones observes Gene in an alley, near a garage door, at 3 o'clock one cold winter morning. Jones asks: "Who are you? What are you doing here?" Gene makes no reply. Jones then notices the garage door has jimmy marks on it, and he sees a screw driver on the ground. Gene's silence, taken into consideration with all the other circumstances, furnishes reasonable grounds to arrest Gene for attempted burglary.

Example

Officer Green made a proper "stop and frisk" of Ed. He politely began to ask some questions, when Ed replied, "I am a law student; I don't have to answer your questions and I'm not going to". Unless there are other circumstances justifying an arrest, this reply, in and of itself, would not authorize Green to arrest Ed.

SECTION D. FORCE PERMISSIBLE IN "STOP-AND-FRISK"

An officer may use reasonable minimal force in executing a "stop and frisk"; he may never use force that is likely to cause death or grave bodily harm.

Example

While Officers Bob and Bill were making a "stop and frisk" of two juvenile robbery suspects in front of a pool hall, the two juveniles started to run away. Bob and Bill chased the youths, caught and tackled them. This police conduct was proper. However, it would have been improper for the officers to fire their revolvers at the fleeing suspects.

SECTION E. "STOP-AND-FRISK" LEGISLATION

Although the right of a police officer to conduct a "stop-and-frisk" is not conditioned upon legislative authorization, "stop-and-frisk" legislation is nevertheless desirable in that it minimizes the necessity for a case-by-case determination of the powers of the police and the rights of the citizens. Several states already have statutes upon the subject and more are considering such enactments.

Following is a draft of a model "stop-and-frisk" statute which was prepared and distributed by *Americans for Effective Law Enforcement, Inc.*, a national, non-partisan, non-political, not-for-profit, tax exempt educational corporation based in Chicago:

A MODEL STATE STATUTE ON "STOP AND FRISK"

§ 1. Whenever any peace officer of this state encounters any person under circumstances which reasonably indicate that such person has committed, is committing, or is about to commit a criminal offense, he may detain such person.

§ 2. Such detention shall be for the purpose of ascertaining the identity of the person detained and the circumstances surrounding his presence abroad which led the officer to believe that he had committed, was committing, or was about to commit a criminal offense, but no person shall be compelled to answer any inquiry of any peace officer.

§ 3. No person shall be detained under the provisions of § 2 of this Act longer than is reasonably necessary to effect the purposes of that subsection, and in no event longer than 15 minutes. Such detention shall not extend beyond the place where it was first effected or the immediate vicinity thereof.

§ 4. If at any time after the onset of the detention authorized by § 1 of this Act, probable cause for arrest of the person shall appear, the person shall be arrested. If, after an inquiry into the circumstances which prompted the detention, no probable cause for the arrest of the person shall appear, he shall be released.

§ 5. Whenever any peace officer authorized to detain any person under the provisions of § 1 of this Act reasonably believes that any person whom he has detained, or is about to detain, is armed with a dangerous weapon and therefore offers a threat to the safety of the officer or another, he may search his person to the extent necessary to disclose, and for the purpose of disclosing, the presence of such weapon. If such a search discloses a weapon or any evidence of a criminal offense it may be seized.

§ 6. Nothing seized by a peace officer in any such search shall be admissible against any person in any court of this state unless the search which disclosed its existence was authorized by, and conducted in compliance with, the provisions of this Act.

When this model statute was sent by *Americans for Effective Law Enforcement* to the Governors, Attorneys General, and legislative officials in January, 1969, it was accompanied by a "position paper" upon the subject. It is herewith reproduced for the consideration of police officers who may wish to promote "stop-and-frisk" legislation in their own jurisdictions:

"STOP AND FRISK"
Position Paper #2
of
Americans for Effective Law Enforcement, Inc.

On June 10, 1968 the Supreme Court of the United States, in *Terry v. Ohio* (and two companion cases), declared that the police practice of "stop and frisk", when properly used, was constitutionally permissible. In other words, it does not constitute an unreasonable search and seizure within the meaning of the Fourth Amendment of the Constitution of the United States. This is the conclusion *Americans for Effective Law Enforcement* had urged upon the Court in the amicus curiae ("friend of the court") brief which it had filed in that case.

Legislation in conformity with the *Terry* case decision is needed in all of the states in order to avoid the uncertainty of a case-by-case adjudication of the powers of the police and the rights of the citizens. Accordingly, AELE has prepared and is distributing to governors, attorneys general, and legislative leaders throughout the country a model "stop and frisk" bill for their consideration.

An appreciation of the need for "stop and frisk" legislation and a proper understanding of the nature of the practice requires answers to the following questions: What is a "stop and frisk"? How does it differ from an arrest and search? When may it be employed by the police? What is the risk of police abuse?

The Meaning of "Stop and Frisk"

The following hypothetical case discloses the meaning of "stop and frisk":

Two police officers are on a routine beat patrol at 3:00 A.M. in a residential neighborhood. It is dark and the streets are deserted. As the police car proceeds down an alley, the figure of a man is seen. He steps to the side, behind a telephone pole. The police car speeds up, and when the officers arrive at the scene they find a man dressed in dark nondescript clothing, standing next to a garage. For all the police know at that moment, he might be a householder who owns the garage—or he may be a recently paroled burglar; he may live next door—or he may live miles away; he may be able to give a good explanation for being there—or he may be prepared to tell a demonstrably false story.

In our hypothetical case three things are clear: (a) the actions of the man are suspicious; but (b) there is no probable cause to *arrest* him for the commission of a *crime,* and yet (c) the police ought to *do something.* The question is, what should they do? What can they do? Are they forced to choose between doing nothing, proceeding on their way, or falsely arresting the suspect for a "crime".

If the officers do nothing, a burglar, robber or rapist might be left in the alley to proceed with his plan unhindered. If the officers make an arrest, the arrestee may turn out to be an innocent resident of the neighborhood, who will thereafter have a police record. Moreover, even if developments subsequent to an actual arrest establish that the suspect was in fact plotting a crime, or had committed one unknown at the time of his arrest, a gun or other evidence obtained from him may be excluded from usage in court because of an arrest made without the constitutional requirement of "probable cause".

Because of these various difficulties, proper police investigative technique demands the employment of another procedure —a middle ground approach—one between police inaction and illegal action. What is needed is the employment of an authorized "stop and frisk" procedure. In this hypothetical case, for instance, the police officers would stop their car, alight from the vehicle and ask the suspect such questions as "Who are you?" "What are you doing in the alley?" "May we see some identification?" The officers must also have the right to frisk the suspicious person if they reasonably think that he may be armed with a dangerous weapon.

Necessarily, the right to ask the questions includes the power to temporarily detain the suspect, even against his will, for a brief time. Since a suspect could defeat the whole purpose of stop and frisk simply by walking away from the inquiring police, under "stop and frisk" authorization he will not be privileged to do so.

Since even a brief detention is a "seizure" of the person within the meaning of the Fourth Amendment of the Constitution, it must be "reasonable", that is, based upon some identifiable and objective standard of suspicion of criminal behavior. It cannot be based upon an officer's whim, caprice, prejudice or inarticulated "hunch".

Suppose that the suspect in our hypothetical case refuses to answer questions asked by the police. He cannot, after all, be compelled to do so, and he may take advantage of his Fifth Amendment right to say nothing. What then? Does this destroy the value of the "stop and frisk" power? The answer is a sure "no", because a quick investigation of the surrounding area may provide enough evidence to give the police probable cause to arrest him for a criminal offense. For example, suppose that in shining their flashlights on the door of the garage next to which the suspect was found the police find fresh "jimmy" marks. They would then have probable cause to arrest the suspect for attempted burglary. If, upon searching him after the arrest, they find a jimmy, or screwdriver that matches the marks on the door, another burglar may well be on his way to the penitentiary.

Even when the police are forced to release the suspect because of his refusal to answer questions or because no evidence of an attempted crime is found at the scene, the very act of temporary detention and questioning may deter, at least for that night, a potential criminal act of violence. That, in itself, would be a worthwhile result, since the duty of the police is not only to apprehend persons who have already committed criminal acts, but also to prevent crimes from occurring in the first place.

Moreover, in many instances a person stopped under circumstances such as the one involved in our hypothetical case will respond to the questions asked by the police; and his answers may supply the necessary information either to dispel the police suspicion or else escalate the suspicion into probable cause for an arrest.

"Stop and frisk" may be used in a number of fact situations: for instance, a teenage boy walking from car to car and apparently testing the windows or looking in for keys left in ignition locks; the person who furtively and repeatedly looks into the window of a business establishment about to close; the man who has been trailing two teenage girls for several blocks. The possibilities are numerous.

The Objections to "Stop and Frisk"

The charge has been made by some persons that "stop and frisk" is a tactic for the repression of minority groups; that it is a racist practice designed to keep the ghetto resident "in his place"; and that it is a tactic to show the teenage gang member, the addict, and the prostitute who "rules the turf" on the officer's patrol beat.

As with all other professions or occupations, there are some policemen who do not deserve the honor of a police badge and the privilege of carrying a gun—just as there are misfit doctors, unethical and incompetent lawyers, and corrupt public officials. On occasions some police, in all parts of the country, have used the power of their office to engage in various kinds of illegal and coercive practices. But that fact does not warrant the withholding of needed authorization to those police officers who do conform to proper standards, and who must have such authorization for the protection of the public and also for their own safety.

The Answer

The basic answer to the concern over possible police abuse of the power of "stop and frisk", as well as of all the other powers the police possess, is the development of better procedures for the selection of police applicants, so as to reject the psychological misfits, the ones whose past conduct evidences a lack of the required integrity, and those whose social values are incompatible with the role of protector of all members of our society.

Adequate compensation must be provided in order to attract applicants with the required qualifications, and to retain in office those who are selected.

Proper internal supervision will also be needed, along with meaningful sanctions for the police who misuse the powers of their office.

Chapter 12

The Self-Incrimination Privilege:

Compulsory Surrender of Physical
Evidence by Accused Persons; and
Indirectly Compelled Testimony

As stated earlier, in the discussion of interrogations and confessions (Chapter 10), the police cannot compel a person to talk to them regarding an offense for which he is a suspect. Any confession obtained by compulsion, either physical or psychological, is void because of its involuntary nature. Moreover, any evidence derived from an involuntary confession is not usable in court.

Legal controls also exist for the purpose of restraining other forms of compulsion on the part of all governmental officials, governmental bodies, and the courts as well. The principal control stems from the constitutional privilege against self-incrimination, as embodied in the Fifth Amendment to the Constitution of the United States. It is available to suspected and accused persons at such functions as coroner's inquests, legislative hearings, and, of course, in judicial proceedings.

SECTION A. HISTORY AND POLICY
OF THE SELF-INCRIMINATION PRIVILEGE

The self-incrimination privilege, in contrast to the involuntary confession rule, was not created for the primary protection of the innocent. It arose out of an early practice in England whereby persons suspected of heresy were brought into the church courts and ordered to speak up as to the charges made against them. A sufficient feeling of opposition to this practice gradually developed so

124

that the church courts ultimately quit doing this. Shortly thereafter, the law courts felt impelled to discard the practice of compelling testimony. In other words, no person accused of *any* offense should be compelled to incriminate himself.

In addition to this historical basis for the privilege against self-incrimination, there was another consideration for its acceptance and incorporation into our federal and state constitutions. There was a feeling that the police should be required to search for other and more reliable evidence than what a court or other governmental unit could extract from the lips of the accused.

The self-incrimination privilege, therefore, is founded very largely upon a policy consideration—the sheer distaste of the idea that a person ought to be required to orally incriminate himself.

Section B. Limitations Upon the Privilege— The Procurement of Physical Evidence

In view of the historical origin and the policy reasons in support of the self-incrimination privilege, what, then, are its limitations— or, more specifically, what, if anything, can be obtained from an accused person, either without his consent or by actual compulsion? As a general rule, it may be said that anything of a *physical* nature may be obtained or compelled from an accused person, insofar as the self-incrimination privilege itself is concerned; or, stated another way, anything is thus obtainable short of incrimination by words which are revealing what is on the mind of the accused with respect to a criminal offense.

There is another constitutional prohibition, however, that serves as a restriction upon the procurement of physical evidence by compulsion—the guarantee that no person shall be deprived of his life, liberty, or property without due process of law. This has been interpreted to mean that as regards physical evidence of guilt, it can only be obtained by *reasonable force,* and under *reasonable circumstances.*

Example
   X, arrested for burglary, refuses to permit his fingerprints to be taken. His hands may be held in such a way as to permit the necessary procedure.

Example
   A and B are lawfully arrested for the possession of narcotics. Both put small plastic bags into their mouths. A police

officer holds A's jaw and pulls out a bag. B, however, swallows his. B is taken to a hospital where, over his protests, his stomach is pumped out and the bag is recovered. The narcotics evidence against A would be admitted at the trial; the narcotics evidence against B would be excluded, but upon the basis of a violation of due process rather than because of a violation of the self-incrimination privilege. (This kind of conduct has been described as "shocking to the conscience" of the courts, and thus violative of due process.)

Example

Mr. Motorist is involved in an automobile accident. An investigating police officer suspects that Mr. Motorist is intoxicated, so he takes Motorist to a hospital where a physician is requested to extract, through a hypodermic needle, a sample of blood for the purpose of a chemical test for alcoholic intoxication. Mr. Motorist refuses to consent, but the blood sample is taken anyway, over his mild resistance. The evidence may be used against him.

Following is a list of the kinds of physical evidence that may be obtained without the consent of an arrestee, or by the exercise of *reasonable force* and under *reasonable circumstances:*

1. "Mug" photographs
2. Fingerprints
3. Fingernail scrapings
4. Samples of hair
5. Specimens of blood, urine, or breath
6. Objects concealed in body cavities, even in the anus or vagina

He may also be required to:

7. Permit the removal of clothing to be searched for concealed items such as narcotics or jewelry
8. Permit an inspection of his body for tattoo marks, scratches, etc.
9. Try on articles of clothing (e.g., a hat left at scene of crime)
10. Appear in a police line-up for identification purposes
11. Speak for purposes of voice identification by witnesses to an offense
12. Provide specimens of his handwriting (e.g., in an extortion or kidnapping case).

In general it may be said that if the evidence sought from the person of the accused is of a *physical* nature, it may be lawfully obtained *without consent*, or *by the use of reasonable force and under reasonable circumstances.*

Even where the evidence comes from the mouth, or through the voice, of the arrestee (or through some other voluntary act on his part), no violation of the self-incrimination privilege is involved, just so long as it is to be used only for its physical characteristics, rather than for its value as *testimony.* For instance, if an arrestee is ordered to utter the words "stick em up", so that a robbery victim can compare his voice with that of the robber, the evidence thus obtainable is of a physical nature only. The same is true of a specimen of handwriting that the arrestee may be ordered to furnish; it is solely for the purpose of a comparison between its *physical characteristics* and those of the document in question (e.g., a ransom note, or a forged check). On the other hand, of course, the arrestee cannot be compelled to furnish a specimen of his handwriting in the form of a statement of his whereabouts at the time of the crime. Similarly, with respect to photographs taken without consent, or over protest or resistance, they must not be in the form of a reenactment of the crime to which the arrestee may have confessed, because in any such reenactment his movements will convey his thoughts and therefore become the equivalent of verbal expressions.

Section C. Indirectly Compelled Testimony

Indirectly compelled testimony, as well as directly compelled testimony, is protected by the self-incrimination privilege. A good, appropriate example of this is the case where a police officer is summoned to testify before a grand jury investigating police corruption. He is advised (1) that anything he says might be used against him in a criminal proceeding; (2) that he has the privilege of refusing to give answers that would tend to incriminate him, but (3) that, by statute and departmental rules, if he refused to answer he would be subject to removal from office. He testifies. Then he is indicted for a criminal offense and his grand jury answers are sought to be used against him. The United States Supreme Court has held that since the officer had no choice between testifying or losing his job, he was indirectly compelled to testify, in violation of his privilege against self-incrimination. His answers to the grand jury, therefore, were not usable as evidence against him upon his criminal trial.

The Supreme Court has also held that a police officer cannot be fired for refusing to sign a waiver of his self-incrimination privilege when summoned to testify before a grand jury investigating corruption in the police department. On the other hand, the Court has said that if an officer is summoned to testify before a grand jury and he refuses to answer questions *"specifically, directly, and narrowly relating to the performance of his official duties"*, the privilege against self-incrimination would be no bar to his dismissal from the police force.

Example

A grand jury is investigating illegal gambling in the community. Captain Tracy is summoned to testify. He is advised of his right to refuse to testify but he is also told that a refusal will necessitate his dismissal from the force. He then testifies and admits that he accepted $500 a month from the gambling operators to overlook their violations. He is later prosecuted for bribery. His grand jury testimony cannot be used against him because he was indirectly compelled to give it, in violation of his self-incrimination privilege.

Example

Captain Knight receives a summons from the same grand jury that called Tracy. Knight is asked to sign a waiver of his self-incrimination privilege before answering any questions before the grand jury. He refuses and is dismissed from the force. His dismissal is invalid, as violative of his privilege against self-incrimination.

Example

Captain Kidd is summoned before the same grand jury. He is not asked to sign a waiver, although he receives the usual warning about his privilege against self-incrimination. He is then asked whether he had received money from Gambler X in return for overlooking X's violation of the gambling laws. Kidd refuses to answer. His refusal would justify his dismissal from the force.

The distinction between the last example and the two preceding it, and particularly the second example, may not be too clear to the reader. He may find comfort, however, in the fact that the distinction did not seem very clear to two of the Justices who had dissented from the original viewpoint of the majority in the United States Supreme Court case from which the first example was drawn.

Chapter 13

The Prohibition Upon Police Entrapment

Out of consideration for the frailties of human nature—the general notion that "every man has his price"—the courts have established the principle that if the police *entice or induce* a person to commit a crime he should not be punished for what he did. The feeling prevails that but for the police persuasion and the temptation the individual may have remained an honest, law-abiding citizen. Accordingly, the courts have provided him with the defense of "entrapment", which means, in effect, he is granted immunity for what he did as a result of police encouragement. On the other hand, if the police merely afford a person an *opportunity* to commit a crime then he has no such defense.

> *Example*
>   Police Detective Healy suspects that Paul is a burglar, but he has never been able to "get the goods" on Paul. One day Healy, posing as an ex-con, has a conversation in a bar with Paul. Healy tells Paul that he can make an easy score at the home of Banker A, who is taking his wife to the opera that night. Healy tells Paul how to gain easy access to the home. Paul accepts the advice with gratitude. Then Healy arranges for a group of police officers to close in just as Paul breaks into Banker A's home. Paul cannot be convicted of burglary; he has the defense of entrapment because Healy, a police officer, *enticed and induced* him to commit the act; the idea did not originate with Paul.

> *Example*
>   A police informant, Lloyd, tells Officer O'Flaherty that a burglar acquaintance of his is planning on breaking into the

home of movie star Crosby next Monday night, a night which he selected because he heard that the Crosby family would all be attending a party elsewhere that night. Indeed the Crosby family had such plans. The police arrange, however, to station three officers in the Crosby home Monday afternoon and remain concealed there after the Crosbys leave. Shortly after they left Lloyd enters the home and is immediately apprehended. He does not have the benefit of the defense of entrapment. He was only afforded the *opportunity* to carry out his plans. It was his own idea, not that of the police.

Example

Druggist Rex is suspected of selling narcotics unlawfully. The police arrange for a known addict, Alex, to try to make a "buy" from Rex. Alex is given marked money and he goes to Rex and asks if he can buy a "fix" of heroin. Rex said he could let him have one for $20. Rex hands the heroin to Alex, and Alex gives him the marked money. After Alex gets out of the store and the substance is verified to be heroin by field testing, the officers enter the store, arrest Rex and find the marked money in the cash register. This is not entrapment. Rex was only given an *opportunity* to make the sale; he was not enticed or induced to do so.

Chapter 14

Eye-Witness Identification—
Police Line-Up Procedures

As discussed earlier, evidence of a physical nature may be obtained from an arrestee without his consent, or, under certain conditions, even over his objection. The same is true with regard to a viewing of an arrestee by the victims or witnesses to a crime; he cannot prevent such a viewing by invoking the self-incrimination privilege. However, there is another constitutional right that is available to him in this situation—his right to counsel.

The Sixth Amendment to the Constitution of the United States provides that in "all criminal prosecutions, the accused shall enjoy the right . . . to have the assistance of counsel for his defense". This provision has been interpreted to mean that, in state as well as federal criminal cases, any accused person is entitled to counsel not only at his trial but also at any "critical stage" of the investigation of the crime for which he is suspected. And the identification viewing process has been held by the Supreme Court to be a "critical stage". The underlying reason for this conclusion is that, without an attorney to observe the eye-witness identification procedures employed by the police, an unfair viewing may occur, perhaps even unrealized by the accused himself; and neither he nor his attorney would be able to disclose that fact or have it revealed at the trial. For this reason, a suspect similar in description to that furnished by witnesses should not be placed in a line-up with other persons totally dissimilar in description to that given by witnesses, for otherwise he would stand out "like a sore thumb" and this would amount to a strong suggestion that he must be the culprit and an identification is in order to provide the necessary proof of guilt. Another related fear is that perhaps the police, thoroughly confident of a suspect's guilt, might resort to various other forms of unfair suggestibility to witnesses, and thereby induce an identification of the suspect that would not otherwise have occurred.

In the decisions which laid down the right to counsel rule, the United States Supreme Court said, however, that this right was one that a suspect could waive. The Court also said that it was not foreclosing the police or the legislatures from establishing various line-up viewing procedures that would insure fairness to the suspect equivalent to, or even better than, the protection that counsel's presence might afford. Presumably a sound movie of the proceeding might be an acceptable alternative.

The Line-Up

Before placing a suspect in a line-up, he should be told (1) that a "line-up" is planned; (2) that he has no legal right to refuse to participate; but (3) that he has a right to have an attorney present during the line-up, and (4) if he cannot afford an attorney one will be afforded him free.

If the suspect states that he does not desire the presence of counsel, he should be asked to sign a waiver to that effect. If he states that he wants counsel, the line-up should be postponed until an attorney can be present.

When counsel is present he is entitled only to observe what occurs; he has no right to ask questions of the witnesses or to do anything other than observe.

In all instances where witnesses are to view a suspect in the station house, the suspect should be placed in a line-up with other persons of the same color and similar in all other essential respects.

The consequences of a violation of any of the safeguards required by the Supreme Court may be the rejection of the identification evidence obtained either at the time of the viewing of when presented in the courtroom by a witness whose courtroom identification may have stemmed from what occurred at the station house line-up.

In all probability a line-up will not be considered necessary when

    (a) the suspect is still at the scene of the crime; or
    (b) the witness knows the suspect personally and has stated that the person he knows is the one who committed the offense; or

(c) if the victim is in danger of death and may not survive long enough for a line-up viewing; or

(d) the suspect asks that he be immediately confronted with the victim or other witness.

Whenever the (d) situation arises, the suspect should nevertheless be advised of his right to a line-up and counsel, and a waiver should be noted in the police records of the case.

Every police department should distribute written instructions to its personnel to assure that the court decreed safeguards are followed. (Samples of the instructions that have been prepared by a number of departments may be obtained by writing to the Director of the Police Legal Advisor Training Program, Northwestern University School of Law, Chicago, Illinois 60611.)

Chapter 15

Electronic Surveillance

In 1968, Congress passed a law making it a criminal offense for *anyone, without proper authorization,* to employ any electronic, mechanical, or other device, to

(1) tap a telephone or intercept any other wire communication, or

(2) intercept other oral communications which occur upon the premises of, or relate to the operation of a business or other commercial establishment engaged in interstate commerce.

The 1968 federal act also sets out the procedures whereby *federal officers* may be authorized to employ electronic surveillance in the investigation of crime and criminals. The procedures consist essentially of the procurement of a court order specifically authorizing the particularized surveillance desired by the federal investigators. Any federal officer who conducts an electronic surveillance other than through this means (unless he does so under a narrowly defined emergency stated in the statute) is guilty of a criminal offense. The same criminal liability attaches to any other person, including state and local law enforcement officers, who indulges in wiretapping or in the interception (by "bugging", etc.) of other oral communications affecting a business or other commercial establishment engaged in *interstate commerce.*

Since the federal act only prescribed procedures whereby federal officers may secure the required court authorization, it is extremely important that the various states enact their own electronic surveillance statutes in conformity with the federal statute. In the absence
134

of such legislation, there can be no wiretapping at all by state or local law enforcement officers; and under no circumstances can they indulge in any other kind of electronic interception of oral communications affecting *interstate* business operations. The term "interstate business operations" has been very liberally extended to include even a hotel operation.

Any state statute, however, must conform as closely as possible to the federal statute; otherwise the state law would be invalid, by reason of the provision of the Constitution that gives priority (preemption) to federal enactments over any state enactments concerning the same subject matter.

Following are illustrations of the problems confronting state and local law enforcement officers in states without the proper legislation:

Example

   Detectives A and B are investigating the activities of hoodlum X whom they very reasonably believe to be involved in the "juice" racket and in the killings of several juice victims. Ordinary surveillance procedures prove inadequate, so A and B want to put a tap on the wires leading to the private telephone in X's hotel suite, as well as place a listening device within the suite itself. In the absence of a state statute the detectives would have no way to obtain lawful authorization to do either of these things. If they went ahead with their plans they would be guilty of a federal offense.

Example

   Detectives A and B strongly suspect that Y and Z plan their "juice racket" operations every day as they meet on a city park bench. The detectives conceal a transmitting microphone under the bench and pick up incriminating information. The detectives have not violated the federal statute, nor would they be violating any state law unless there was a law prohibiting eavesdropping.

   Whether the evidence obtained by the above means was valid would depend upon the reasonableness of their actions in the light of the constitutional prohibition against "unreasonable" searches and seizures. In this instance the evidence would probably be held to be valid and usable.

Example

   H is also suspected of being involved in the "juice" racket. He owns a very small shirt shop which is known to the police

as a meeting place for juice racketeers. Detectives A and B
arrange to get into the shirt shop one night and plant a concealed microphone therein. They pick up incriminating information against H.

A and B probably have not violated the federal electronic
surveillance statute because the shirt shop could hardly be
classed as involved in interstate commerce. But the evidence
would not be usable because of the constitutional prohibition, both state and federal, against unreasonable searches
and seizures.

With an appropriate state statute, the detectives in all of the three
foregoing examples would be able to procure state court orders
which would render their actions lawful and also render the evidence thus obtained admissible in court.

By way of summary, and to avoid any misconceptions, we wish
to say that in the absence of appropriate state legislation that would
permit the issuance of court orders upon the conditions required by
the federal statute, state and local police officers *cannot:*

1. Electronically tap a telephone or wire communication, or
2. Electronically intercept any conversation in any place involved in interstate commerce.

However, if there is no state statute specifically forbidding electronic surveillance, state and local police officers *may* indulge in such
a practice with regard to communications other than those over a
telephone or wire facility, or other than in a place affected with interstate commerce, and the evidence obtained can be used in a criminal
prosecution—*provided* the interception was conducted upon *probable cause* and in a *reasonable manner.*

A model state electronic surveillance statute, conforming to the
requirements of the Constitution and to the federal statute, has been
prepared and distributed to the Governors, Attorneys General, and
to legislative leaders in all fifty states by the educational corporation, *Americans for Effective Law Enforcement, Inc.*

Part IV

CRIMINAL AND CIVIL LIABILITY OF LAW ENFORCEMENT OFFICERS

A police officer who abuses his law enforcement powers may be liable both civilly and criminally before state and federal courts. This part of the book will discuss the various types of legal proceedings in which he may become involved, and their consequences.

Chapter 16

State Criminal Liability of the Police

It is elementary that a police officer is not immune from criminal prosecution. The elements of many criminal offenses are such that an erring police officer might well fall within their scope.

Following are some of the criminal offenses for which a police officer can be prosecuted for acts committed while serving as a police officer:

1. Intimidation

A police officer who threatens to detain and question a relative of an accused in order to induce the accused to cooperate would be guilty of intimidation.

2. Extortion

A police officer who threatens a person with arrest or with physical brutality in order to procure money from that person would be guilty of extortion.

> *Example*
> A police officer threatens a prostitute with arrest or physical violence unless she pays him a certain amount of money each week. The officer is guilty of extortion.

3. Coercing a Confession

Some states have laws which make it a crime to obtain a confession by means of physical force or threat of physical force.

> *Example*
> A police officer, in attempting to extract a confession, tells the accused that unless he cooperates some other police

officers who are not as sympathetic as the questioning officer might physically abuse him. The crime of coercion has been committed.

4. Assault and Battery

A police officer who threatens to abuse an accused may be guilty of the crime of assault. If his threat is carried out, the offense of battery would occur.

5. Electronic Surveillance

Some states have laws against electronic surveillance (electronic eavesdropping and wiretapping). However, in a majority of states electronic surveillance (as opposed to the tapping of a telephone line) is permissible when one party to the conversation has given consent to the eavesdropping, and in such situations a recording by the police officer is permissible.

6. Possession of Unauthorized Deadly Weapons

Although most police officers are permitted to carry concealed pistols, knives, and other weapons that an ordinary citizen is not permitted to carry in a concealed manner, there are certain weapons that even a police officer, in most jurisdictions, is not permitted to carry. Usually listed among these prohibited weapons are gun silencer, sand-clubs, metal knuckles, switch-blade knives, and sawed-off shotguns.

7. Aiding Escape

It is a crime to help any prisoner escape from custody. A police officer who turns his back on an escaping prisoner would be guilty of this offense.

8. Perjury and Subornation of Perjury

A police officer-witness who knowingly testifies falsely in a criminal trial commits perjury. If the officer induces a witness to testify falsely, the officer is guilty of the crime of subornation of perjury.

In both crimes, the false statement must be made under oath and it must be material to the issue before the court. Also, the police officer must know that the false statement is not true.

9. Communicating with or Harassing Witnesses or Jurors

It is a crime to harass or coerce a juror or witness in regard to his participation in a criminal trial. Thus, a police officer who attempts to coerce a witness not to testify would be guilty of this offense. Also, a policeman who attempts to influence a juror improperly would fall within this provision.

10. Bribery

It is a crime to offer or to accept a bribe. A bribe is something of value offered or accepted with the intention of influencing official performance. For example, a police officer who accepts a "gratuity" from a motorist in order to give the motorist a "pass" is guilty of bribery. Similarly, a police officer who offers a bribe to another public official would be guilty of the offense.

11. Failure to Report a Bribe

The statutes of many jurisdictions require a public official to report an attempted bribe to the prosecutor or the chief of police. Failure to do so constitutes an offense. A police officer who fails to report an attempted bribe to his appropriate supervisor would be guilty of this offense.

12. Tampering with Public Records

It is an offense to destroy, tamper with or remove a public record. Therefore, a police officer who wrongfully alters a station's booking record or removes an arrest record violates this provision.

13. Official Misconduct

By state statute it is a crime for a public official to knowingly exert his official authority to the detriment of another in an unlawful manner. For example, a policeman who uses his office in order to collect money for a private collection firm would be guilty of official misconduct.

14. Violating Rights of Accused

Many states have recently adopted legislation providing for criminal penalties against law enforcement officers who violate specified statutory rights afforded to a person accused of a crime. For example, a police officer who refuses to permit an accused to call his attorney may fall within this provision.

Although the instances of prosecution of police officers under state criminal statutes are not frequent, there is no question as to their applicability to errant police conduct. Moreover, in most states the commission of any of these offenses, whether prosecuted or not, constitutes grounds for discharge of the officer from the force.

Chapter 17

State Civil Liability of the Police

There are three types of civil tort cases which are frequently filed against police officers in connection with the performance of their duties. These are actions for (1) false arrest and false imprisonment, (2) malicious prosecution, and (3) negligence.

1. False Arrest—False Imprisonment

Since arrest and custody usually occur contemporaneously, actions for false arrest often contain an additional count for false imprisonment. False imprisonment is the unlawful restraint of an individual's personal liberty or freedom of movement.

In addition to being a part of a false arrest transaction, false imprisonment may occur independently of a false arrest. This might occur in a situation where there is probable cause to make the arrest, but later investigation indicates that the arrested person did not commit the crime and should be released. The police officer who persists in detaining the arrested person under these circumstances may be liable for false imprisonment, but only in those states which permit an officer to release an arrestee without a court order to that effect.

143

2. Malicious Prosecution

Malicious prosecution occurs when a police officer knowingly signs a complaint or causes a complaint to be signed against a person whom he knows did not commit the crime.

Malice is an essential element of malicious prosecution. The prosecution of a person with any motive other than that of bringing a guilty party to justice is a malicious prosecution. Malicious prosecution is not established merely by the fact that the party bringing the suit was acquitted of a criminal charge. Malice may be inferred from lack of probable cause, but will not be inferred where probable cause exists, and it will not be presumed if all the evidence shows there was no malice. For instance, where a police officer, in good faith, submits the facts fairly to a prosecuting attorney and obtains his advice with respect to a person who is supposed to have committed some offense, and the police officer acts on the advice given by the prosecuting attorney and causes proceedings of a criminal nature to be instituted against the arrested person, such facts will constitute a complete defense to an action for malicious prosecution, although the person charged is not, in fact, guilty.

3. Negligence

A police officer who injures someone through ordinary negligence during the course of his official duties could be sued successfully in a civil proceeding. For example, a police officer who attempts to apprehend a suspect and fires his weapon negligently, thereby injuring an innocent bystander, would be subject to civil liability. Negligent conduct through use of police vehicles also would subject an officer to this type of civil liability.

4. Indemnification of Police Officer

A police officer is primarily liable for any judgment obtained against him. This means that he must pay out of his own pocket any money awarded to the person who successfully sues him. However, some jurisdictions have enacted indemnification statutes or ordinances. This type of legislation provides that the state, city, or county, as the case might be, will reimburse the police officer for any money damages awarded against him *arising out of* conduct performed in the course of *his official duties*. A policeman, however, is never reimbursed under an indemnification statute or ordinance if his wrongful actions were "willful or wanton" misconduct. A willful or wanton act under the law is one which shows a deliberate intention to harm, or shows an utter indifference to or a conscious disregard for the safety of others.

Example

A police officer, without any pretense of legal justification, physically abuses an individual. The officer would not be reimbursed for any money damages secured against him. Likewise, an officer who injures persons or property on a high speed "joy ride" in a squad car would not be entitled to indemnification. But a police officer who injures a person through ordinary negligence in a traffic accident would be entitled to indemnification.

Chapter 18

Federal Prosecution and Federal Civil Liability Under the Civil Rights Act

1. Criminal Liability of the Police

The Federal Civil Rights Act provides for criminal prosecutions of police officers who deprive citizens of any federal right under the United States Constitution or federal law. This federal prosecution is a corollary to the remedy of civil suit available to the victim of police misconduct under the Federal Civil Rights Act.

The most frequently invoked provisions of the Federal Civil Rights Act is that portion which reads as follows:

> "Whoever, under color of any law, statute, ordinance, regulation of custom, willfully subjects any inhabitant of any State, Territory, or District to the deprivation of any rights, privileges, or immunities secured or protected by the Constitution or laws of the United States, or to different punishments, pains, or penalties, on account of such inhabitant being an alien, or by reason of his color, or race, than are prescribed for the punishment of citizens, shall be fined not more than $1,000 or imprisonment not more than one year, or both."

Example
> A police officer who tries to beat a confession out of a suspect.

Example
> A police officer who unlawfully searches an apartment without a warrant and without grounds for a search incident to an arrest.

Example
A police officer who prohibits an individual from passing out religious pamphlets in a reasonable manner.

Example
A police officer who, in making an arrest, uses excessive force because the arrested individual is a member of a minority group which the police officer does not like.

Criminal prosecution, like civil liability under the Federal Civil Rights Act, is limited to state, county, municipal and other local law enforcement officers. Federal law enforcement officers are excluded from criminal prosecution under the Act, with one exception: District of Columbia police officers, although not civilly liable under the Act, are subject to criminal prosecution under the Civil Rights Act.

Another Federal Civil Rights Act criminal provision often invoked reads as follows:

"If two or more persons conspire either to commit any offense against the United States, or to defraud the United States, or any agency thereof in any manner or for any purpose, and one or more of such persons do any act to effect the object of the conspiracy, each shall be fined not more than $10,000 or imprisoned not more than five years, or both.

"If, however, the offense, the commission of which is the object of the conspiracy, is a misdemeanor only, the punishment for such conspiracy shall not exceed the maximum punishment provided for such misdemeanor."

Still another section of the Civil Rights Act provides for criminal prosecutions for conspiracy. Police officers, as well as private persons who conspire with them, are subject to prosecution under this provision.

Example
A citizen loaned money to individuals at a high rate of interest, and received a note as evidence of the loan. When the note was not paid on time, Citizen A hired Police Officer B to collect the amount owed. Police Officer B, in uniform, visits the borrower, threatens arrest, and beats the borrower in order to collect the monies owed to Citizen A. Both Citizen A and Police Officer B are subject to prosecution under the Civil Rights Act.

2. Civil Liability of the Police

Since a landmark decision of the United States Supreme Court in 1961 (*Monroe v. Pape*), the Federal Civil Rights Act has been used with increased frequency by private citizens seeking to recover damages against police officers for alleged wrongs received during the course of police performance. The provision of the Federal Civil Rights Act most frequently invoked in these cases reads as follows:

> "Every person who, under color of any statute, ordinance, regulation, custom, or usage, of any State or Territory, subjects, or causes to be subjected, any citizen of the United States or other person within the jurisdiction thereof to the deprivation of any rights, privileges, or immunities secured by the Constitution and laws, shall be liable to the party injured in an action at law, suit in equity, or other proper proceedings for redress."

The Federal Civil Rights Act may be invoked against a state, county, municipal or other local police official. It may not be invoked, however, against a federal law enforcement officer.

> *Example*
>
> A federal narcotics officer and a state police officer make a narcotics raid together. During the narcotics raid they perform an unreasonable search and seizure and also beat the person in whose apartment the raid occurred. The state police officer can be sued, but the federal narcotics officer is immune from such suit. However, the federal officer could be sued civilly.

✿   ✿   ✿

In order to sue under the Federal Civil Rights Act the conduct which is the subject of the law suit must have been performed by the police officer "under color of" his official position. This means that if the police officer performs a wrongdoing in the conduct of his duties as an officer, even though his conduct is beyond the scope of his proper duties, or even prohibited by his Department, liability may accrue under the Federal Civil Rights Act. However, when the police officer is clearly acting as a private citizen, he may not be sued under the Federal Civil Rights Act.

> *Example*
>
> Officer Jones on his night off goes to a tavern, drinks too much, engages Citizen A in a fight, and breaks A's jaw. The next day while on duty, irritated by the effect of the drink the night

before, Officer Jones uses excessive force in arresting Citizen B. Citizen B, who did not provoke Officer Jones in any manner, sustains a broken jaw. Citizen B may invoke the Federal Civil Rights Act; Citizen A may not. When Officer Jones struck Citizen B he was acting in his official capacity; Citizen A, however, was struck while Jones was acting as a private citizen. Citizen A, of course, could still sue Officer Jones as a private citizen in a tort action.

The Federal Civil Rights Act may be invoked to collect damages for violation of "rights, privileges, or immunities secured by the (Federal) constitution and laws". However, it does not provide for redress for a violation by a police officer of a state constitution or local law.

Example

Officer Brown arrests Citizen B. A state statute provides that upon making an arrest an officer must bring the arrested person before a magistrate within a two hour period. Officer Brown delays three hours before bringing Citizen B before a magistrate. During that period Citizen B was not interrogated by the police; nor was any other unlawful conduct performed. B may not sue Officer Brown under the Federal Civil Rights Act. Officer Brown deprived Citizen B of a right secured under a state statute, but not under federal law or the United States Constitution.

The Federal Civil Rights Act provides for every type of relief available under the law. This means that the relief need not be limited to money damages.

Example

Citizen D owns and operates a book store. The local ladies "Do-Good" organization thinks that Citizen D sells "dirty" books. The police have examined these books and determined that they are not legally obscene. However, the president of the ladies "Do-Good" club is married to Officer White who is assigned to the police district where citizen D's book store is located. Every morning Officer White, at the behest of his wife, goes to Citizen D's book store, searches for the "dirty" books and seizes the books which his wife has told him about. Citizen D may file a Federal Civil Rights Act against Officer White and, in addition to collecting money damages, may enjoin Officer White from coming into the book store and harassing him.

Chapter 19

The Personal Liability of Prosecuting Attorneys

A judge or magistrate has judicial immunity from civil suits arising out of any judicial action, even though the judicial action was erroneous and to the detriment of the potential plaintiff. Similarly, a prosecutor enjoys immunity for any legal action he takes or initiates in his official capacity.

> *Example*
>
> Prosecutor Pete erroneously charges Carl with grand larceny when the value of the goods taken by Carl only warranted, at most, a prosecution for petty larceny. Carl pleads guilty and is sentenced. Later both Carl and Pete discover the error. Carl cannot sue Pete successfully because of Pete's immunity for legal actions taken as a prosecutor.

A prosecutor, however, is liable for "non-legal" activities in which he may involve himself. This is a problem for rural prosecutors who often perform some functions which are more akin to police work than legal activity.

> *Example*
>
> Prosecutor Jim leads an obscenity raid of police officers on Sam's Store. Jim seizes certain allegedly obscene books himself and directs police officers to seize others. Subsequent events prove (a) the search to be unlawful, (b) the books not to be obscene, and (c) the suffering of damages by Sam for loss of unreturned merchandise and for loss of sales because of the wrongful closing of his store. Sam sues Jim for money damages under the Federal Civil Rights Act. Jim defends by invoking immunity of a prosecutor. Jim's defense

is without avail. His actions in regard to Sam's Store were not those of a prosecuting attorney but rather of a police officer; consequently, Jim was not clothed with immunity.

A prosecutor, like a police officer, is not immune from the criminal laws.

Example

Dan was a witness for the prosecution. Just before trial he decided not to testify. Prosecutor John attempted to get Dan to testify by breaking a few of his limbs. John would be guilty of the crime of battery, and a special prosecutor would have to be appointed to prosecute him.

Appendices

Appendix A

CONSTITUTIONAL PROVISIONS OF PARTICULAR IMPORTANCE TO THE POLICE

Preamble

We the People of the United States, in Order to form a more perfect Union, establish Justice, insure domestic Tranquility, provide for the common defense, promote the general Welfare, and secure the Blessings of Liberty to ourselves and our Posterity, do ordain and establish this Constitution for the United States of America.

Article I

. . .

Section 8. The Congress shall have Power To lay and collect Taxes, Duties, Imposts and Excises, to pay the Debts and provide for the common Defence and general Welfare of the United States; but all Duties, Imposts and Excises shall be uniform throughout the United States; . . .

To regulate Commerce with foreign Nations, and among the several States and with the Indian Tribes; . . .

To provide for the Punishment of counterfeiting the Securities and current Coin of the United States; . . .

• • •

To define and punish Piracies and Felonies committed on the high Seas, and Offences against the Law of Nations;

To declare War, . . . and make Rules concerning Captures on Land and Water; . . .

To provide for calling forth the Militia to execute the Laws of the Union, suppress Insurrections and repel Invasions;

To provide for organizing, arming, and disciplining, the Militia, and for governing such Part of them as may be employed in the Service of the United States, reserving to the States respectively, the Appointment of the Officers, and the Authority of training the Militia according to the discipline prescribed by Congress;

To exercise exclusive Legislation in all Cases whatsoever, over such District (not exceeding ten Miles square) as may, by Cession of particular States, and the Acceptance of Congress, become the Seat of the Government of the United States, and to exercise like Authority over all Places purchased by the Consent of the Legislature of the State in which the Same shall be, for the Erection of Forts, Magazines, Arsenals, dock-Yards, and other needful Buildings;—And

To make all Laws which shall be necessary and proper for carrying into Execution the foregoing Powers, and all other Powers vested by this Constitution in the Government of the United States, or in any Department or Officer thereof.

Section 9.

. . .

No . . . . ex post facto Law shall be passed.

* * *

Article III

Section 1. The judicial Power of the United States, shall be vested in one supreme Court, and in such inferior Courts as the Congress may from time to time ordain and establish. The Judges, both of the supreme and inferior Courts, shall hold their Offices during good Behaviour, and shall, at stated Times, receive for their Services, a Compensation, which shall not be diminished during their Continuance in Office.

Section 2.

. . . the supreme Court shall have appellate Jurisdiction, both as to Law and Fact, with such Exceptions, and under such Regulations as the Congress shall make.

The Trial of all Crimes, except in Cases of Impeachment, shall be by Jury; and such Trial shall be held in the State where the said Crimes shall have been committed; but when not committed within any State, the Trial shall be at such Place or Places as the Congress may by Law have directed.

Section 3. Treason against the United States, shall consist only in levying War against them, or in adhering to their Enemies, giving them Aid and Comfort. No Person shall be convicted of Treason unless on the Testimony of two Witnesses to the same overt Act, or on Confession in open Court.

* * *

Article VI

. . .

This Constitution, and the Laws of the United States which shall be made in Pursuance thereof; and all Treaties made, or which shall be made, under the Authority of the United States, shall be the supreme Law of the Land; and the Judges in every State shall be bound thereby, any Thing in the Constitution or Laws of any State to the Contrary notwithstanding.

. . .

AMENDMENTS

Amendment I

Congress shall make no law respecting an establishment of religion, or prohibiting the free exercise thereof; or abridging the freedom of speech, or of the press; or the right of the people peaceably to assemble, and to petition the Government for a redress of grievances.

Amendment II

A well regulated militia, being necessary to the security of a free State, the right of the people to keep and bear arms, shall not be infringed.

Amendment III

No Soldier shall, in time of peace be quartered in any house, without the consent of the owner, nor in time of war, but in a manner to be prescribed by law.

Amendment IV

The right of the people to be secure in their persons, houses, papers, and effects, against unreasonable searches and seizures, shall not be violated, and no warrants shall issue, but upon probable cause, supported by oath or affirmation, and particularly describing the place to be searched, and the persons or things to be seized.

Amendment V

No person shall be held to answer for a capital, or otherwise infamous crime, unless on a presentment or indictment of a Grand Jury, except in cases arising in the land or naval forces, or in the militia, when in actual service in time of war or public danger; nor shall any person be subject for the same offence to be twice put in jeopardy of life or limb; nor shall be compelled in any criminal case to be a witness against himself, nor be deprived of life, liberty, or property, without due process of law; nor shall private property be taken for public use, without just compensation.

Amendment VI

In all criminal prosecutions, the accused shall enjoy the right to a speedy and public trial, by an impartial jury of the State and district wherein the crime shall have been committed, which district shall have been previously ascertained by law, and to be informed of the nature and cause of the accusation; to be confronted with the witness against him; to have compulsory process for obtaining witnesses in his favor, and to have the assistance of Counsel for his defence.

* * *

Amendment VIII

Excessive bail shall not be required, nor excessive fines imposed, nor cruel and unusual punishments inflicted.

Amendment IX

The enumeration in the Constitution, of certain rights, shall not be construed to deny or disparage others retained by the people.

Amendment X

The powers not delegated to the United States by the Constitution, nor prohibited by it to the States, are reserved to the States respectively, or to the people.

* * *

Amendment XIV

Section 1. All persons born or naturalized in the United States, and subject to the jurisdiction thereof, are citizens of the United States and of the State wherein they reside. No State shall make or enforce any law which shall abridge the privileges or immunities of citizens of the United States; nor shall any State deprive any person of life, liberty, or property, without due process of law; nor deny to any person within its jurisdiction the equal protection of laws. . . .

Section 5. The Congress shall have power to enforce, by appropriate legislation, the provisions of this article.

Note

The first eight Amendments are known as the *Bill of Rights*. They were originally intended, and at one time judicially interpreted, as restrictions upon the federal government alone, and not the states. In recent years, however, the Supreme Court has held that a number of the provisions of the *Bill of Rights*—those that the Court considers essential to "fundamental fairness" in criminal trials—are applicable to the states by virtue of the guarantee in the Fourteenth Amendment that *no state* shall deprive any person of life, liberty, or property, without "due process of law."

An illustration of the application of the foregoing line of reasoning is the so-called "exclusionary rule"—the court-developed rule that requires the rejection of evidence that has been obtained by an "unreasonable" police search or seizure.

When originally created, the exclusionary rule was a rule of evidence, required only by federal courts in *federal cases*. It was not conceived as a constitutional requirement; the states, therefore, were at liberty to adopt or refuse to adopt the rule, and they ultimately were about evenly divided with respect to this choice. Later on, however, the Supreme Court elevated the exclusionary rule into a constitutional requirement, just as though it had been written into the Fourth Amendment after the stated prohibition against "unreasonable searches and seizures". In the 1961 case of *Mapp v. Ohio,* the Court held that the Fourth Amendment's protection and the exclusionary rule were elements of "due process" and therefore binding upon all the states. As a consequence, no state court may now admit, in a criminal case, evidence secured as a result of an "unreasonable" search or seizure. And just about any "illegal" search or seizure will be considered to be an "unreasonable one".

Appendix B

COMPLAINT FOR ARREST

STATE OF ILLINOIS ⎱ ss.
COUNTY OF COOK ⎰

THE CIRCUIT COURT OF COOK COUNTY

—————————— ——————————
(Court Branch)   (Court Date)

The People of the State of Illinois
          Plaintiff

COMPLAINT

    V.

No. _____

———————————————
        Defendant

_____complainant, now appears before
(Complainant's Name Printed or Typed)
The Circuit Court of Cook County and in the name and by the authority of the People

of the State of Illinois states that _____
                                    (defendant)

has, on or about _____ at _____
               (date)   (Place of offense)

committed the offense of _____ in that he
                             (offense)

_____

_____

_____

in violation of Chapter_____ Section_____
ILLINOIS REVISED STATUTE AND AGAINST THE PEACE AND DIGNITY OF
THE PEOPLE OF THE STATE OF ILLINOIS.

———————————————————
(Complainant's Signature)

——————————————— ——————————
(Complainant's Address)   (Telephone No.)

STATE OF ILLINOIS ⎱ ss.
COUNTY OF COOK ⎰

———————————————————
(Complainant's Name Printed or Typed)
being duly sworn, on _____ oath, deposes and says that he has read the
foregoing complaint by him subscribed and that the same is true.

———————————————————
(Complainant's Signature)

Subscribed and sworn to before me _____, 19_____.

———————————————————
(Judge or Clerk)

I have examined the above complaint and the person presenting the same and have
heard evidence thereon, and am satisfied that there is probable cause for filing same.
Leave is given to file said complaint. Warrant issued.

Bail Fixed at $_____

Judge _____

Appendix C (1)

ARREST WARRANT

THE CIRCUIT COURT OF COOK COUNTY, ILLINOIS

The People of the State of Illinois
Plaintiff

V.

_____
Defendant

_____ _____
(Court Branch)   (Court Date)

ARREST WARRANT
THE PEOPLE OF THE STATE OF ILLINOIS TO ALL PEACE OFFICERS IN THE STATE —
GREETING:

We command you to arrest _____
(Defendant)

for the offense of _____ stated in a
(offense)

charge now pending before this court and that you bring him instanter before The

Circuit Court of Cook County at _____
(location)

or if I am absent or unable to act before the nearest or most accessible court in Cook
County or if this warrant is executed in a county other than Cook, before the nearest
or most accessible judge in the county where the arrest is made.

Issued in Cook County_____, 19_____

Bail fixed at $_____

_____
Judge

WITNESS: _____ CLERK OF THE COURT

and the Seal thereof, at Chicago _____

_____ 19_____

_____
Clerk

160

Appendix C (2)

BACK SIDE OF ARREST WARRANT FORM

Case No._____

INFORMATION AND DESCRIPTION OF DEFENDANT

Name _____ Alias _____

Residence _____ (Apt.) _____

Sex	Race	Weight	Height	Birth Date	Age	Complexion	Build	Mustache	Glasses
				(Day-Mo.-Yr.)					

Place of Employment _____

Occupation _____

Address _____

Soc. Sec. No. _____

Hours of Employment _____

Additional Information _____

Complainant's Name _____

Residence _____ Tel. No. _____

Where Employed _____ Address _____ Tel. No. _____

Additional Information _____

By order of the Court, the officer making the arrest is required to notify the complainant.

Criminal _____ No. _____

THE CIRCUIT COURT OF
COOK COUNTY

THE PEOPLE OF THE STATE OF ILLINOIS

V.

_____

ARREST WARRANT

Filed _____, 19____

_____
                Clerk

Complainant _____

Address _____

Telephone No. _____

Officer _____

161

Appendix D

A CONCISE FORM OF COMPLAINT FOR ARREST, FOR USE IN MASS ARREST SITUATIONS, AS IN RIOTS OR OTHER CIVIL DISTURBANCES

_____   _____
(Court Branch)   (Court Date)

MISDEMEANOR—AGGRAVATED ASSAULT ON A PEACE OFFICER

STATE OF ILLINOIS ⎱ ss.   THE CIRCUIT COURT OF COOK COUNTY
COUNTY OF COOK ⎰

The People of the State of Illinois,   COMPLAINT
_____ Plaintiff,
                                              No. _____
         vs.   Defendant.

_____, complainant, now appears before the Circuit
   Complainant's name printed or typed
Court of Cook County and in the name and by the authority of the People of the State
of Illinois states that _____ has, on or about _____
                              Defendant   Date
at _____, Cook County, Illinois, committed the offense
   Street Address   City
of Aggravated Assault in that he, while committing an assault on _____,
                                                                  Name of Victim
that is without lawful authority he engaged in conduct which placed _____
                                                                     Name of Victim
in reasonable apprehension of receiving a battery, knew the said _____
                                                                  Name of Victim
to be a peace officer of the _____
                              Name of Police Department
engaged in the execution of his official duties, in violation of Chapter 38, Section
12-2(a) (6), Illinois Revised Statutes, AND AGAINST THE PEACE AND DIG-
NITY OF THE PEOPLE OF THE STATE OF ILLINOIS.

_____
Complainant's Signature

_____
Complainant's Address   Telephone No.

STATE OF ILLINOIS ⎱ ss.
COUNTY OF COOK ⎰   _____
                          Complainant's Name Printed or Typed

being first duly sworn, on his oath, deposes and says that he has read the foregoing
complaint by him subscribed and that the same is true:

_____
Complainant's Signature
Subscribed and sworn to before me _____, 19_____.

_____
Judge or Clerk

ORDER FOR WARRANT	ORDER FOR LEAVE TO FILE COMPLAINT (ARREST WITHOUT WARRANT)
I have examined the above complaint and the person presenting the same and have heard evidence thereon and am satisfied that there is probable cause for filing same. Leave is given to file said complaint. Warrant to issue.	I have examined the above complaint. Leave is given to file said complaint.
Bail fixed at $_____	Bail fixed at $_____
Judge_____	Judge_____

Appendix E

COMPLAINT FOR SEARCH WARRANT

_____ _____
(Court Branch)   (Court Date)

STATE OF ILLINOIS ⎱ ss.   THE CIRCUIT COURT OF COOK COUNTY
COUNTY OF COOK ⎰

COMPLAINT FOR SEARCH WARRANT

_____ complainant
now appears before the undersigned judge of the Circuit Court of Cook County and
requests the issuance of a search warrant to search the person of _____

_____ and

_____
(Premises, City and State)

and seize the following instruments, articles and things:_____

_____

_____

_____

which have been used in the commission of, or which constitute evidence of the
offense of _____

    Complainant says that he has probable cause to believe, based upon the follow-
ing facts, that the above listed things to be seized are now located upon the (person
and) premises set forth above:

_____

_____

_____

_____
                                  Complainant

Subscribed and sworn to before me on _____, 19____

_____
                            Judge

163

Appendix F

SEARCH WARRANT

State of Illinois   }
County of Cook   }   ss.

                        The Circuit Court of Cook County

The People of the State of Illinois to all peace officers of the state.

Search Warrant

    On this day _____, Complainant has subscribed and sworn to a complaint for search warrant before me. Upon examination of the complaint, I find that it states facts sufficient to show probable cause.

    I therefore command that you search _____
                                                (Person)

and _____
              (Premises)   (City and State)

and seize_____
          (Instruments, Articles, and Things)

_____

_____

_____

_____

which have been used in the commission of or which constitute evidence of the offense

of _____

    I further command that a return of anything so seized shall be made without unnecessary delay before me or before Judge _____, or before any court of competent jurisdiction.

                                                _____
                                                    Judge

Time and date of issuance _____

About the Authors

FRED E. INBAU
Fred E. Inbau is Professor of Law at Northwestern University and a former Director of the Chicago Police Scientific Crime Detection Laboratory.

MARVIN E. ASPEN
Marvin E. Aspen is Head of the Appeals and Review Division of the City of Chicago Law Department, and former Assistant State's Attorney, Cook County, Illinois.